"Antong Lucky's story is about transformation from beginning to end. Every human being has a God-given inalienable right to enter the road to redemption. He's the example of the redemption our nation needs."

—Malik Aziz, chief of police of Prince George's County, Maryland

"With breathtaking candor, Antong Lucky shares his compelling journey from devastating poverty and incarceration to neighborhood leader in low-income Dallas communities, becoming a nationally recognized activist, equipping and empowering young inner-city residents, and advocating for sweeping changes in urban power structures to create a more just society. Antong has an extraordinary gift for leadership and a heart for community service. His story will inform and inspire others. It could very well change your life."

—Don Williams, founder and CEO of the Foundation for Community Empowerment

"Antong Lucky's story is both wrenching and inspiring. His experience is an undeniable lesson in how people can transform themselves, each other, and their communities in ways the criminal legal system never can."   —Danielle Sered, author of *Until We Reckon: Violence, Mass Incarceration, and a Road to Repair*

"Experience an intellectual marvel tell a miraculous true story that provides the solution to the widening divides in America. Antong Lucky reveals harsh realities and presents compassionate activism for timeless hope and a renewal of the belief that fearless love will win."

—Drew Willey, CEO and founder of Restoring Justice

"*A Redemptive Path Forward* is both timely and timeless. Antong's profoundly moving memoir offers a searing portrait of a young man caught between the laws of America's unjust legal system and the laws of the streets—both hell-bent on cutting his life short before it really even begins. Yet above all else, Antong gifts us with his inspiring journey to redemption. Hope is fuel, and this important book delivers it in droves—just when we need it most."
—Brittany K. Barnett, attorney and author of *A Knock at Midnight: A Story of Hope, Justice and Freedom*

"Reading this book, *A Redemptive Path Forward*, has given me insights into just how vulnerable our youths are. The streets are waiting to pull them in. Antong's redemptive path is masterfully laid out as a guide for others to follow. His natural leadership is turning this idea of redemptive activism into a force for good to be reckoned with!"
—Alice Marie Johnson, criminal justice activist, author of *After Life: My Journey from Incarceration to Freedom* and CEO of Taking Action for Good

"Antong's redemptive journey from the most dangerous man in his neighborhood to an ambassador of peace should be required reading for anyone who wants to understand what authentic transformation truly requires. Over the years, I have had the privilege of witnessing first-hand his trials and tribulations, but more importantly, his many, many triumphs."
—Bob Woodson, President of the Woodson Center

A
REDEMPTIVE
PATH FORWARD

From Incarceration to a Life of Activism

ANTONG LUCKY

Counterpoint
Berkeley, California

A REDEMPTIVE PATH FORWARD

Library of Congress Cataloging-in-Publication Data
Names: Lucky, Antong, author.
Title: A redemptive path forward : from incarceration to a life of activism /
Antong Lucky.
Description: First hardcover edition. | Berkeley, CA : Counterpoint Press, 2022.
Identifiers: LCCN 2021027663 | ISBN 9781640095342 (hardcover) | ISBN
9781640095359 (ebook)
Subjects: LCSH: Lucky, Antong. | Ex-convicts—Texas—Dallas—
Biography. | Ex-gang members—Texas—Dallas—Biography. | African
American men—Texas—Dallas—Biography. | African American
prisoners—Texas—Dallas—Biography. | African American social
reformers—Texas—Dallas—Biography. | Criminal justice,
Administration of—United States.
Classification: LCC HV9468 .L83 2022 | DDC 365/.6092 [B]—dc23/
eng/20211228
LC record available at https://lccn.loc.gov/2021027663

Jacket design by Jakarie Ross
Book design by Wah-Ming Chang

COUNTERPOINT
2560 Ninth Street, Suite 318
Berkeley, CA 94710
www.counterpointpress.com

Printed in the United States of America

1 3 5 7 9 10 8 6 4 2

I dedicate this memoir to my friend, my brother, father figure, and spiritual guide, the late Bishop Omar Mulidna Jahwar. Twenty-one years we spent together, each and every single day epitomizing and advocating Redemption & Transformation for the least of thee. If I had to do it again, I would choose you. Thank you for believing in me. May your soul rest with the greats who also fought to make this world a better place.

I've come to understand and to believe that each of us is more than the worst thing we've ever done.

—BRYAN STEVENSON, TED TALKS, MARCH 5, 2012

Redemption is possible, and it is the measure of a civilized society.

—GREG BOYLE

CONTENTS

FOREWORD

After nearly two decades of friendship co-laboring, my friend, my brother, MY FAMILY, Kiddo Antong Lucky, delivers us a memoir that gives us an inside look at his transformational journey. The epitome of redemption and transformation himself, this memoir captures a step-by-step and process-by-process layout of this journey and provides a comprehensive glimpse into the fortitude it takes to bounce back from the crushing idea of the hood that so many young men in urban communities find themselves trapped under.

This book is the TRUTH for communities, prisons, schools, and nonprofits across this nation. It not only provides real evidence that transformation exists, but is also an inspiring blueprint for those trying to find a way out. A brother who ran a gang now helps kids stay out of gangs. A brother who ran from police now trains and works with police. TRUTH.

As a father, a brother, a coach, and, most important, a man of God, I personally recommend this book to anyone looking for inspiration and motivation. This is the real-life story of an underdog who became the big dog that helps the little dogs' perspectives on their transformational journey.

—Deion "Prime Time" Sanders, Pro Football Hall of Fame NFL Player and 2021 Southwestern Athletic Conference Coach of the Year

INTRODUCTION

EVERYTHING MUST CHANGE

I was born in 1976 in an East Dallas housing project named Frazier Courts, a low-income housing project with a reputation that said: *Enter at your own risk.* Frazier Courts was filled with drugs, alcohol, and violence, with little hope for anyone ever getting out. It was one of the toughest neighborhoods in Dallas. Nobody flinched at the sound of a gunshot; nobody startled at the sight of the police cuffing someone on the street. The underground culture of the neighborhood was etched into the value system and maintained by a seemingly inextinguishable loyalty to it. The flashes of hope came in the form of education and the earnest attempts of educators who saw something in the kids and made every attempt, despite the odds, to bring it out of them. School was a refuge for me and many other young people who sought to escape the harsh realities of our environment and sometimes even the war zones of our own homes. As much of a star as I was in school early on—I was a straight-A student—it was no match for the pressures of the hood. Survival was the rule of law.

Twenty years later, I was in prison as a direct result of a life spent acting out the ideas and images impressed upon me during my childhood and formative years in East Dallas. In prison, I had time to stop and realize how much Frazier Courts and its surrounding neighborhood had played a significant role in not only my being there but also the hundreds of thousands of kids like myself, born and raised in the hood, who eventually end up in a jail cell—or the grave. Was this the only fate for us or was there something else at play?

Twenty more years have passed since I got out of jail, and the changes I've made are evidenced by the fact that I am a father, mentor, youth advocate, and public speaker, as well as a community and redemption activist, meaning that I believe every single person is worthy of setting right the mistakes they've inevitably made along the way. Likewise, many things have shifted in America over the past two decades. Whether it's race relations, the office of the president, social media, technology, or the way that music is made, transformation is visible all around. But one thing that has stubbornly *not* changed is my old neighborhood, the one that gave birth to the destructive ideas that almost ruined my life—the one that put me at risk for an early death and helped pave my path to prison. It is also the same neighborhood that issued fatal blows to many of my homeboys. Respect to: Rodney Bennett, Stephen Harris, Marvin Sneed, Edward Tate, William Herndon, Sparkle Watson, Cedrick Derrett, Brandon Chew, and Bobby Irvin—rest in Paradise. It issued those same blows to many of my enemies too. I carry them all in my mind and heart.

There is an old song—many have recorded it, but Nina Simone offers the most memorable rendition—that echoes an even older, agreed-upon social principle: "Everything must change." But if this is true, then how is it that change never seems to come to the hood? "No one, no one stays the same," Simone sings in her unique, heart-wrenching way. But even if the people change—*even as I myself have changed*—Frazier Courts stubbornly stays the same. The expectations for prison or death are *still* as they've always been. The dropout rate is *still* steadily rising. It is *still* an impoverished, drug-infested, violent environment; if it is true that *everything* must change, the hood is long overdue.

In the past, the responsibility for making change happen has been left to politicians, police, or pastors. Occasionally, an inspired civil servant would try to facilitate change—but as soon as funding stopped, so too did the endeavor. While signs of hope do occasionally flicker forth from these efforts, the hood is still, in equal parts, dysfunctional, depressing, and dangerous. East Dallas is no exception.

Political representation over the last forty years, despite its various earnest attempts, has not changed the high rates of incarceration, addiction, run-down properties, and poverty. Policing is still a contentious process, to say the least, causing too many Black citizens to be unfairly harassed, arrested, shot, and murdered. This has grown ever more apparent over the last decade, the ubiquitous smartphone making it possible for almost every citizen to catch a hideous array of police brutalities on video. I don't think anybody will soon forget the unflinching gaze of Officer Derek Chauvin, hand in pocket as if to prove how casually he took his power, while he pressed his knee into George Floyd's neck for *more than eight minutes*. Meanwhile, many good police officers find themselves on the retaliating end of the responses to these unrelenting brutalities perpetrated against unarmed African Americans. Simultaneously, crimes in lower-income neighborhoods are reported in disproportionately higher numbers than other areas; one in every three adult males from these neighborhoods is either on probation, parole, or in prison. A staggering 82 percent of those killed or incarcerated as youths are from these severely impoverished urban communities.

Of course, there are those, like me, who are born in the hood and manage to make it out alive and relatively unscathed by the turmoil. But the fact is that there are far more victims than survivors. In comparison to those living in middle- or upper-class neighborhoods, the risk is greater for people in the hood to realize and perpetrate violence; to be unemployed or underemployed; to be poorly educated, if educated at all. The possibility of becoming an addict or imprisoned is far higher than in any other community in America.

For the last two decades, urban neighborhoods, schools, and juvenile detention centers have consistently fed a pipeline to prisons across America by failing to meet the needs of children from these environments. I was one of them. Neither schools nor the juvenile system are able to redirect defeated young boys like me. Strict discipline—without any regard for the situation or circumstances we might be in—is typically used to try to rewire or retrain kids like myself. No one cared about my living situation or what I faced going to and from school, walking the streets of the hood. How can you expect a kid to focus when he is either getting beat up or bullying others—and you *will* find yourself on either one side or the other—on the way to and from school?

These neighborhoods, by and large, have been the origin of most of the people put in jail during the mass incarceration era of the last two decades—which has since been proven ineffective in deterring crime. I believe in consequences for breaking the law and bad actions; however, I also believe that, given the circumstances most kids encounter in the hood—a barrage of difficulties that start coming at them from the moment they are born into this world—we need a new approach that takes into account the dysfunction and trauma suffered in these broken communities.

The need for change now is required if we are going to reverse the effects of an overcriminalized society rife with senseless violence and the young people who come out of it with no regard or empathy for human life. I had the same attitude as a kid. Throughout my childhood, I secretly, shamefully, longed for a mentor who could understand what I was going through. *Secretly* because it would have felt too vulnerable to admit that I wanted this kind of help and *shamefully* because I understood that I needed to be as rough and reckless as everyone around me if I was going to survive. It seemed naive—or worse, weak—to wish for someone to help me get out of the wasteland of my neighborhood. And so, like most kids in the hood today, I was misunderstood from the get-go—and mislabeled a delinquent. We need an influx of mentors in these areas to create a change that will profoundly affect the mind, heart, and soul.

During the Clinton Administration's "Super Predator" era—when the 1994 crime bill was introduced and the White House espoused the idea that Black communities ought to be disciplined with harsh punishment rather than supported with welfare—many young people and fathers were removed from the community and put in prison. As a result, many single mothers were left behind to raise the kids on their own. We are now experiencing the impact of those decisions with a generation of kids in urban neighborhoods brought up in families stripped of all support. Fathers in jail; mothers at work; kids left to their own devices, growing up in the shadow of a society that had been trained to view them suspiciously rather than with compassion and imagination. We all have a role to play in helping individuals have a better life. In doing so, we also help families, communities, cities; the change ripples outward until, finally, the entire nation has changed.

Now, after forty years of looking the other way, it is time to reexamine our approach to changing the hood. Growing up as the oldest child of a single mother, watching her struggle, I was left only with my sheer spirit to live. And, thankfully, I was able to not only survive but also eventually hoist myself up into a better life. I am not a politician, pastor, or paid civil servant—I am just one person who beat the odds and is alive today to tell his story with the hope of moving us forward.

I managed to stagger through as a kid, hone my instincts and develop my knowledge in prison with the unexpected time I found in there, and then use my experiences as a way to create best practices for healing our communities, working with children, former gang members, *and* the police in the hood. Through redemption activism, we can produce decent tax-paying citizens, a well-informed society, and a better understanding of law enforcement, community development, and reinvestment. Only then will we be able to address police brutality, racism, and reverse racism and find a path toward ending mass incarceration.

Let me show you a redemptive path forward with the story of a child born as Antong Glenn Lucky.

A
REDEMPTIVE
PATH FORWARD

I

———————◆———————

THE BOY IS THE FATHER OF THE MAN

I am a product of love. I was born to two people at a time in their lives when such a thing seemed possible. In 1976, my mother, Inez Lucky, was madly in love with my father, William Hinton. She was sixteen and he was seventeen. They were passionate enough to believe that their relationship would endure the pressures of poverty and the statistical realities for young poor people who drop out of school to become parents.

The first year of my life, the three of us were inseparable. My father was proud to have a family and my mother was doing everything she could to be a good mom and hold her man down. No matter how "good" the love was, though, the reality of being teenage parents was a bitter one. Between diapers, formula, baby clothes, and the rare time for privacy that young people crave—not to mention the crime and violence that was raging just outside the door—the struggle became far too real, far too quickly. My father became a hustler, making money by any means necessary, in order to provide. Hustling eventually evolved into full-fledged criminal activities. Just over a year into their relationship, when I was one year old, my father was convicted of aggravated robbery and sentenced to fifty years in prison.

Coming up, I never knew the details of why my father was arrested. I often heard family members defensively brush off his arrest, saying that he didn't commit the crime. No one seemed interested enough to relay the full story of his absence, so I was left in limbo, trying to figure it out on my own—which caused me to suppress and bury most of my questions about him. The only sure way of learning anything about my father was eavesdropping on conversations between the adults. I would listen in on my mother chit-chatting with her friends in our living room. "Man, Glenn, he didn't take no mess," one of them would say to my mother, "but he sure did love you. He would do anything for you." Sometimes I would even hear things in the streets from people who recognized me as my father's son and would occasionally mention some miniscule memory of him, usually something that illustrated how tough he was and how respected he was for that in the hood.

As a child, I lived off those moments. Trying to know my dad through this odd assemblage of interactions—strangers making small talk about our resemblance or my mother making a scold out of my father when she punished me for a misdeed, "looking like your daddy with his no-good ass"—was all I had. Believe it or not, those were some of my best memories. But even though something inside of me would always want to hear more about him, something else inside of me wouldn't allow me to ask for more. It was foolish pride: trying to avoid the embarrassment that I would inevitably feel for not knowing anything about this person responsible for my existence. Still, I gathered from my eavesdropping and street encounters that I must have something of my father's spirit because I too was quiet, fearless, and bold.

Left to raise me on her own, my seventeen-year-old mother applied for the necessary aid from the state welfare program and public housing, designed to help a struggling family get back on their feet. As a result, she was able to move into her own place in Frazier Courts. Even to this day, Frazier Courts is the home of countless single mothers who are, like my mom was, not yet legal adults and have no choice but to sacrifice their own ambitions and dreams to figure out a way to take care of their children. My mother struggled and worked long hours to make ends meet. She barely had the time or energy to tend to me after a hard day of work. She did the best she could; I can appreciate this now. She dropped out of school to raise me—because who else could she turn to for help?

I was a Lucky through my maternal bloodline; my mother gave me her last name. That side of my family had a ruthless reputation that encompassed all of East Dallas. As children, our minds unwittingly store certain bits of information that are a part of the household; these bits of emotional ephemera can slowly become romanticized. For me, those were the stories, mostly told by my uncles, of somebody getting beat down, shot, or killed.

I was about three or four when my uncle Lonnie's body was brought home from prison in a box. I remember we all went over to see him in my grandmother's living room. I was lifted up and held over the casket so I could see his expressionless face. That whole night, there was story after story about how bad Uncle Lonnie was, how many people he had beaten, fought, and chased through the streets. Those memories were told in a way that made me proud of Uncle Lonnie and proud of all of my other uncles who were so strong and unafraid. There were also rumors that Lonny had been killed by Black building tenants—*building tenants* are prison inmates given certain privileges over the others; they act as minor correctional officers. Imagine being killed in prison by another Black man acting out on orders from the guards. After my uncle's burial, I never heard anyone talk about that again.

Three years after my father went to jail, my mother met another man who stepped in and became my stepdaddy—Booker T, named after the great educator and author who called for Black progress through education and entrepreneurship over a century ago. My stepdaddy was nice at the onset, but six years and two siblings later—my brothers were born in 1980 and 1983, respectively—he, too, succumbed to the inescapable pressures of poverty and raising a family. I watched helplessly as he and my mother began to fuss and fight more and more. Later in life, I found out that Booker T had been my father's friend. With him away in prison, I think I was a reminder of my father to both of them. Maybe the guilt my mother felt for being involved with one of my father's friends drove her to take her frustration out on me at times.

When I was ten, my mother left Booker T amidst their constant struggles and soon after met a seemingly nice guy, Michael Kenneth Joseph. He had an East Coast accent, real proper seeming. I believed my mother could finally be happy with this man, free of fighting and arguing. And I wanted so badly for my mother to be happy. It was like I could always feel her pain, carrying her outsized struggles as I did in my small frame. Michael had odd jobs here and there, but he also always did the cooking and cleaning, and he played some good music while my mother was at work. He attempted to be a father figure, giving my brothers and me advice, trying to beat back the bad ideas of East Dallas knocking at our door. I remember one Christmas, Mike and my mother woke us up and gave us all gifts of nice clothes, which we badly needed. I felt so proud that we'd had a carefree Christmas and I was finally able to sport some new outfits to school. Michael was also the first man to take my brothers and me to church. My mother worked long hours as a caregiver at the CC Young Nursing Home and was too tired most of the time to take us to church. But every Sunday morning, with the smell of breakfast in the air, she always had some church music blasting through the speakers.

By that time I was a teenager, and crack cocaine had torn a hole in our community, ravishing everything and everyone. Mike was no exception. I don't know when he started using, but I can still see the pain in my mother's eyes as she came to understand that he was free-basing. She started noticing things missing from the household: a TV, the VCR, some cassette tapes, whatever item Mike might be able to magically transform into crack. I listened through the walls many nights as my mother pleaded with him to get help. I hated seeing her go through this situation again. Most of my mother's days were spent taking care of elderly white men and women, from feeding and clothing them to changing diapers. The work was undesirable, to say the least, but she never complained. Then, after a long day, she would come home and prepare us a decent meal. Our household was the neatest one in our neighborhood; when we acted out of line, my mother punished my siblings and me by having us clean the baseboards with a toothbrush. She instilled in us a crucial sense of discipline but also a feeling of protection; we knew she would provide for us no matter what.

Eventually, after another son and a daughter were born, when I was fifteen years old, my mother decided to move on from Michael. She loved him, but his addiction had taken its toll on their relationship. Now, looking back, of course, it's easier for me to understand

the adult strains everyone was under; I don't blame my mother or
Booker T or Michael for the rocky times we had. On the whole, I felt
well cared for in what were sometimes excruciating circumstances,
and I admire their grit.

And, perhaps most crucially, my grandfather, Emmitt Lucky,
had always been a father figure in my life. He was a hard-working
disciplinarian who valued family. He worked for Dallas Water Util-
ities for three decades until his retirement; he was extremely disciplined about his money. He was the only homeowner of the family,
and he lived in a more desirable area on Frazier Street. This gave
me dual citizenship of sorts. While only walking distance from
each other, these two areas—where my mother lived and where my
grandparents lived—were marked by invisible boundaries; one was a
proper middle-class community and the other was the hood. I had
the freedom to roam in both because I was a Lucky, which had its
own particular cachet in Frazier Courts. Since my grandparents
were homeowners, I also had access to an area that otherwise would
have been off limits. I preferred my grandparents' house—it was a
calmer place to be, but also I felt I got more love, or perhaps just less
complicated love, from my grandparents.

My grandfather always greeted me with a smile and often with
his prediction that I would be a preacher one day. "Antong, you've
got what it takes to lead us," he would say, swelling me with a sense
of self-importance. His wife, my grandmother, Thelma Lucky, was
the backbone of our family. She was an incredibly loving and warm
woman, and all of her grandkids longed to be with her all of the time.
Even when she'd call us into the house from a day of playing outside
and give us castor oil—which we all hated but she insisted was good
for us. I was her favorite and given the esteemed privilege of sleeping

in the bed with her whenever our mothers would leave us in her care when they went out and partied. My brothers and cousins had to sleep in the back room on pallets with my grandfather.

For all that I didn't have, the Lucky bloodline compensated in some ways. At the ages of six and seven, I didn't know or understand that we were poor or that I was at risk for so many negative outcomes. All I knew and understood was family. For me, at that time, family was everything. There were even times, when I was messing around at my grandparents' house with my brothers and cousins, I would forget the difficulties of my mother's household just around the corner or that I'd lost my father to prison.

My cousins and I did everything together—as we grew older, we came to be known as the Lucky Gang. Up and down Frazier Street, my cousins and I played curb ball, marbles, one-two-three red light, prison bell, and football. As we shared more than just blood, we also began our mischief at that time. We shared being poor, which creates the strongest desire to have what you see—on TV and magazines and in your mind's eye—but never get to taste, feel, and experience. It was like living in a hothouse of deprivation. My cousins and I were convinced that we'd have to carve out whatever pleasure we could, *however* we could. We always wanted quarters to play video games at the local store; we always wanted more to eat and better tennis shoes; we always wanted to go somewhere other than where we were.

And yet at school I was content. I have always loved learning. My uncle Thelton nicknamed me "Blimpy." At first everyone thought it was because I had a big head, but he later told me that it was because I had such a big brain. Coming home with straight As to both my mother and grandmother's smiling faces also made me love doing well in school. The way they valued education and rewarded it never left me.

By the second grade, though, I started to realize that not everybody else my age felt the same way. Getting in a fight was an everyday
thing where I was from—and nobody was exempt, especially not the
A students. I tried not to let on that I got such good grades, but my
cousins knew anyway. They would overhear the family discussing my
report card or the teacher's insistence on moving me up a grade. I
was placed in the Talented and Gifted Program, but after school,
I joined my cousins in bullying the other smart kids in an effort to
differentiate myself.

By the third grade, the Lucky Gang became the most menacing
and ruthless preteen gang in East Dallas. We allowed a few neighborhood kids to join in with us, but mostly it was about bloodline.
We made all the kids at school pay us fifty cents or more a day; when
they didn't, we'd jump them in the bathroom or put somebody's head
in the toilet. I generally tried to stay in the back as a show of support
for my tougher cousins, but occasionally I had to put in the work
myself.

One day after school, when I was nine years old, my cousins
egged me on to fight Rodney, a friend of mine who lived on the same
street as my grandparents and who walked home from school with
us every day. The pressure of appearing "in" with my cousins was
exceedingly strong—so I accepted the challenge. There was a ritual
of putting sticks on the shoulders of two boys; the "baddest one," the
one ready to declare a fight, would knock the stick off the other boy's
shoulder. If this boy didn't respond by knocking the other stick off,
then he forfeited the fight. If he *did* knock it off, that meant he was
agreeing to scuffle; it was like the bell going off in a boxing match. So,
my cousins—most of them older than I was and without an ounce
of empathy left in them by then—arranged to have Rodney and I

face off. I will never forget the confusion in Rodney's eyes as, walking home, my cousins suddenly turned us to face each other, placing a stick on each of our shoulders. Rodney and I stood awkwardly as my cousins began slapping each other's backs, hunched over in laughter, their hands covering their mouths as if they couldn't contain their enjoyment. I felt my true self sink down somewhere deep inside as I conjured a new persona for the fight. I stepped forward and knocked the stick off Rodney's shoulder. Rodney paused for a long while, his eyes darting from me to my cousins, and then halfheartedly knocked the stick off my shoulder. Once we crossed that threshold, though, we were completely in it. Rodney and I were scrappily throwing punches; my cousins were hooting and hollering. "Show your skills, Kiddo!" my cousins, calling me by my nickname, shouted. Rodney and I locked in a contorted embrace, pulling at each other's shirts, spinning uselessly around until, finally, I landed a punch that bust open Rodney's lip. My cousins declared me the winner. I ran home, thinking about how stupid and cowardly I had been for acting on my cousin's taunting but also relieved that I'd won. The next day, Rodney and I met at our usual corner after school and walked home together, his lip swollen and bruised; he mumbled something about still being friends, right?

A month later, my teacher announced to the class that Rodney had drowned in a swimming pool. I half believed that was some kind of punishment for my behavior; that somehow I had upset the natural order of things by fighting Rodney. It was also the first time that I realized, with a sickening thud, what death meant: I would never see my friend again.

2

Hood Credentials

What my cousins and I did to Rodney—and countless others after that in far more serious fights—was unacceptable. It was inhumane. But, sadly, in the hood, it was—and still is—the norm. Unsuspecting bystanders are targeted and beaten in inner cities across America. Some kids are even challenged to take on felony offenses—committing a robbery or shooting someone—in order to gain hood credentials or to become affiliated with a gang. For boys, initiation entails about a minute of brutal brawling in the middle of a circle of onlookers; for girls, there is a similarly degrading rite of passage, including fighting and sometimes performing sexual acts, in order to "prove" they are legitimately hood. It gives kids the feeling of being animals, living in the wild where they must seek out the weak to devour. It is at this point that empathy—and I am speaking of myself here too—begins to grievously erode.

Not long after the incident with Rodney, I was sent to a new elementary school called Edna Rowe, in a neighborhood known as Pleasant Grove. Naively, I hoped that this change of scenery would mean that the antics and shenanigans of the Lucky Gang would soon be coming to an end.

Instead, when I arrived, I learned that the whole school had already heard of the Lucky Gang. While I didn't want the adults and teachers to know that I was part of it, I definitely enjoyed the respect and other perks that came with its reputation. I was surprised to find the other students were clearly intimidated by me. I recognized this because they treated me with the same standoffish reverence I had long held for my older cousins. I began to walk a tightrope, trying to balance these two sides. On one hand, I was still drawn toward getting a good education and receiving hugs, smiles, and praise for being a good student. On the other, I tried to nurture my new reputation as an intimidating leader in the Lucky Gang.

Pleasant Grove was on the "good side" of town; going to school there introduced me to an entirely different culture. There was a diverse array of kids; in class, I sat next to a kid named Abdul from Ethiopia. He was living in an orphanage, the Buckner Home. As our friendship developed, he told me more about his situation, which seemed a thousand times worse than mine. While I didn't have a daddy, he didn't have parents at all and was ridiculed at school because of his accent, shoddy clothes, and for generally being "lame" according to the standards of our culture. Regardless of what the other kids thought about him, he was book smart, and that became the basis of our initial bond. Our friendship remained limited to the classroom—where, as top students, we were equals.

Outside of the classroom, though, I didn't have the compassion or human capacity to admit that Abdul was my friend. One day, as I was coming around the corner from school, I saw that one of my cousins—we called him Rainbow—had jacked Abdul up against a wall and was shaking him down for his allowance. I immediately stepped out of Abdul's line of sight. I felt disgusted that I hadn't been brave enough to use my voice or influence to help my friend. It was a similar feeling as when I had fought Rodney—as if I were being forced to lead a double life. The next day when I saw Abdul, his eye was badly swollen, and I felt my stomach churn.

And yet, even as I was losing the deepest part of myself, I was still having a good time at school. In those days, we all came to Edna Rowe dressed to impress. Those who received the most attention were the ones who wore Adidas, Guess, Filas, Reebok, and the latest Diadora sneakers. Since my uncle Smokey kept his kids in name brand clothes, the entire Lucky clan was able to keep up because we all wore each other's clothes. (Uncle Smokey was a major hustler and character—he used to offer us twenty dollars to peel the dead skin off his feet, among other chores, which we would happily do to line our pockets with the extra cash.) Thankfully, one of Smokey's sons— my cousin, K-Ray—and I were the same size. I remember walking into the school dance—we called it the Sock Hop—in Guess overalls and fresh mountain climber boots with the red fat laces. "Push It" by Salt-N-Pepa started jamming in the background. I wasn't a hardcore dancer—I was too cool for that—but I was, for sure, one of the smoothest dudes in the building.

After the first semester, just as I felt like I was getting the hang of life at Edna Rowe, the schools were redistricted again, and we were suddenly all transferred to yet another school by the name of Pearl C. Anderson Elementary. Although this one was only a couple of miles away from Frazier Courts, it may as well have been in North

Korea. It was an area known as South Dallas—which was Crips territory, a longstanding rival neighborhood to East Dallas.

Unlike at Edna Rowe, the infamous reputation of the Lucky Gang didn't help me at the new school at all. In fact, it seemed to me that the kids at Pearl C. were ready to fight us *because* we were part of the Lucky Gang. And, since we were being brought into their neighborhood, they had the advantage of being on their home turf. To leave the school in the afternoon, we had to rely on the school bus to get us back to the safer territory of Frazier Courts. Unfortunately, the bus was as inconsistent and unpredictable as my grades were starting to become by then. On the days when the bus left without us, we would inevitably have to fight somebody on the walk home. If the South Dallas crowd was just too big for us to take on, we had to make a break for it and sprint all the way home. During that time, I felt like I was always running and looking back behind me to see if we were going to make it to our side of town safely. This led me to my first conspiracy theory: I had to imagine that whoever came up with the idea of having us bused there surely wanted us dead. In the end, I gained nothing academically at that school, but I became a fierce brawler for sure.

Back in our neighborhood, there was a car wash at the edge of the projects that had become *the* place to hang. All the drug dealers got their fancy cars shined up there. On any given day, the place looked like a car show, with loud music blasting from the lineup of Cadillacs. All the hustlers would stand around in the parking lot wearing the latest fashion and oversized jewelry. Next to the car wash was the community swimming pool where all the neighborhood kids hung out. After a couple of hours of swimming, my cousins and I would walk over to the car wash, looking to make some money to buy something to eat.

At first, the hustlers would pull out wads of cash and just give us money to buy something to eat. They would ask about our grades and tell us to stay in school. But we soon realized that if we pitched in and started to really clean up their cars—getting in there and shining up their gangsta white wall tires—they would pay us even more money to do so. The only thing we had to do was invest in our own SOS scouring pads and we were in business.

One day after getting out of the swimming pool, I decided to go across the street to the store and steal some SOS pads so I could make some extra cash. I walked into the store, still soaking wet from the swimming pool; our mothers would've killed us had we taken their good towels out of the house, let alone to the swimming pool, so mostly we just dried off in the sun.

That was my first time ever stealing something from a store, and I have to admit, despite how far down the path I'd already traveled with the Lucky Gang, I was afraid. I shuffled to the back of the store and then hurriedly put the SOS pads in my shorts; I kept my eyes straight ahead the entire time. Then I turned on my heel and started going in another direction, as if I couldn't find what I was in there to buy. As I approached the end of the aisle, an Asian man began yelling at me from behind the counter. He kept asking, "What you got? What you got?" I had no idea what had given me away. I finally shouted, "Nothing!" And he shouted back, "Police!" He started pointing at my waist, so I looked down. Beaming through my soaking wet white shorts in bold blue read the words *SOS Pads*. I had been so nervous that I hadn't even bothered to glance down at myself to make sure the stolen goods had been concealed properly. I ran full speed out the door and kept on going until I was sure that I couldn't be found. After that incident, I vowed I would never steal again—and I didn't.

I did, however, begin showing up at the car wash every day after school and on weekends too. I religiously ducked down behind some cars at around 4:00 p.m. when my mother got off work so she wouldn't see me as she rode the bus past the car wash on her way home from work. She knew that mostly drug dealers hung out there and was adamant in telling me that if she caught me there, I would get a whipping I wouldn't soon forget. I didn't want to disobey her—but the pull of those five- and ten-dollar bills was mighty strong.

One day, one of the better-known hustlers approached my cousins and me and asked if we would like to make twenty dollars a day. Of course, we all said, "Yeah!" He explained that all we had to do was stand at the end of the street—or we could ride our bikes up and down the street—and if the police came by, we were supposed to scream "Headache!" at the top of our lungs. Soon, that was our full-time job. And not long after that, after seeing that we were more dedicated than the other neighborhood kids, we were promoted to selling drugs every day at the carwash.

At that time, crack was everywhere, and money was flying. We couldn't believe—after having been pinned under the heel of destitution for so long—how quickly our fortunes seemed to be changing. When I was twelve years old, I remember a guy showing us how to take Superior B, which was a crystallized B12 vitamin supplement, and cook it so that it would dissolve to look just like crack cocaine— we quickly learned it sold just like it too. We began working for ourselves. Genuine crack can take on three colors: white, yellow, or brown. So we would pour orange juice into our concoction if we wanted to achieve a more authentic yellowish color, or we'd add Coca Cola to give it that distinct brown look. Then we'd add some Orajel—the medication used for numbing toothaches—so that if someone wanted to break off a piece and taste it, their tongue would go numb, as it would with real crack. We would then package our fake product up and sell it; we called it Procaine.

In the end, we would spend only fifteen dollars on Superior B and then easily make a thousand off it. And we basically got away with it—sometimes people complained that our product was weak, but, for the most part, business was booming. And I'd gone from washing the dealers' cars at five dollars a pop to making between five and seven thousand a week selling imitation cocaine. We spent the money as soon as we made it.

I remember a customer pulling into the carwash from Tyler, Texas. He'd heard about our product, and he said he wanted to buy everything I had. When I thumbed through the wad of bills he handed over, I lost count about three times because it was so much money. I finally just said, "It's good," and moved the customer along before he saw me for who I really was: a thirteen-year-old boy who couldn't even keep track of the dough that grown men were handing over for his fake batches of crack cocaine.

Somehow, I didn't hold myself to the same moral standard when it came to selling drugs that I did when I was taking part in the more physical rituals of our gang—beating kids up or brawling with rivals from South Dallas. In part, I justified what I was doing because I saw it as providing not only for myself but also for my family. I'd seen my mother go through so much with her relationships—all of them eventually ending on a dramatically embittered note—and I wanted to be able to be the man of the house, to give her the things she couldn't afford.

The first time I tried to hand over a lump sum of cash to my mother, though, proved to be a very different experience from the one I'd fantasized about for so long. One day, when I was thirteen or so, I gathered a bundle of money; I was excited to help out and show my mom her son had become a man. I waited for my mother to come home from work. When she did, I waited for her to get settled in the kitchen, where she was unpacking groceries and starting to sort things out for dinner. "Here, Mom, this is for you," I said with solemn pride as I handed her a roll of hundred-dollar bills. She looked down at the money in my hand and then up at me, her eyes flashing with unanticipated rage. "Don't you ever offer me drug money in my house again," she said in a barely contained whisper—and then the dam broke. Suddenly she was yelling at the top of her lungs and letting cuss words fly—*"Don't bring that shit into my house!"* She said that if I'd done anything illegal for that money, she didn't want any part of it. I thought she was being stubborn and unfair. Mostly, though, I was taken aback that she had just so harshly punctured the illusion that what I was doing was okay because I had been doing it for her. In hindsight, my mother was my first example of a truly principled person.

I thought I was grown, of course, and knew what I was doing. Outside of my house, I was surrounded by images and ideas of promiscuity everywhere I turn. All my cousins had girlfriends; the older, popular guys had a whole string of women. But I only wanted Kimberly. She was brown skinned, with an athletic build. She had beautiful brown eyes and dimples that appeared every time she smiled at me. Rumor had it that she'd been on the wrestling team at her old school, and she was good at it too. That mix—her sweet smile and fierce skills—made me like her even more.

We lived in the same apartments at Frazier Courts, but Kimberly's mother didn't allow her outside much; she would come home from school and go straight into her apartment. So the only opportunity I had to talk to her was when she brought the trash out. I'd catch Kimberly at the dumpster and try to use our brief time together to convince her that I wasn't like the other dudes in the projects. I'd constantly pressure her for her phone number; eventually she gave in. She also took my phone number and then warned me, in a stern voice, never to call her; she would call me. Her mom didn't want her associating with any of the other kids who lived in the projects. After that, like clockwork each day, I waited by my phone for her call.

Once we started dating, Kimberly and I would talk on the phone into the wee hours of the morning. I would play cassette tapes, singing my heart out to Keith Sweat's "You May Be Young But You're Ready" to her over the telephone. Often, we would both fall asleep while still on the phone. She'd wake up and shout "Kiddo" while pressing the buttons on her phone until finally I'd jump up and say "Huh?" On several occasions, my mother would wake me up because I'd fallen asleep on my mother's plastic-covered couch we were forbidden to sit on, the phone off the hook. Kimberly was my girl, and we were both proud to tell it.

I was thirteen and still a virgin; Kimberly told me that she was too. At night, I would sneak out of the house at 11:00 p.m. when her mother had just left for work as a night shift nurse; then I'd go back home every morning just before 7:00 a.m., when her mother would return. My own mother, asleep the entire time, never even knew I'd been gone. Kimberly and I began our sexual relationship and I quickly fell deeply in love. Or at least I thought it was love. I could tell Kimberly everything that was on my mind, and she would listen attentively, occasionally offering her input. I valued being able to trust someone with my secrets. I think I fell so hard because it was the first time I felt such a pure sense of connection *and* escape. It was a corner of life where I was allowed to be as innocent and full-hearted as I truly felt. I didn't have to be the tough guy the hood wanted me to be; I could drop the façade. Even though I was just a kid, I would often fantasize about the two of us growing old together.

My friends would tease me and say Kimberly had "my nose wide open," meaning she had me right where she wanted me. I was furious whenever someone said those words. It drew me right back into a world where I had to pretend I was something I wasn't; I didn't want that phrase associated with my name. Being in love could put you at risk for more ridicule.

Then, one day, about seven months into my relationship with Kimberly, I was playing basketball with my friends at the court when one of my homies, two or three years older than me, walked over to us. He began to circle our game and say things about how he'd "put hickeys on Kiddo's girl's neck." I could feel the blood rushing to my wildly beating heart; my head felt light. This guy, Arthur, was taunting me—not just for having a girlfriend who would cheat on me but also for falling in love at all. Like: *That shit don't happen here.* "I thought she was your girl?" Arthur asked, still walking round my friends and me as if he were a lion stalking its prey. "Why she let me put hickeys on her neck if that's your girl?" We stopped the game; my friends stared at me to see what I would do. I laughed it off, even though images of him kissing Kimberly's neck, giving her those pas-sion marks, flashed like a nightmarish slide show through my mind. I wanted to throw up. I wanted to rip him apart. Still, something in me held out hope. Something in me said, *Ask her first.*

I ran toward Kimberly's apartment, a thousand thoughts flying through my mind, all of them pointing me in a direction I didn't want to go. I managed to get Kimberly to come outside of her apartment and asked her about what had happened. She said that the two of them had been playing around and he'd held her down, kissing her against her will. For a moment, I had a flickering, hopeful sense that we were going to be able to put all of this nonsense behind us. But then the story changed . . . and changed . . . and changed again. Kimberly was even younger than me—she was twelve years old; neither of us had any idea how to navigate a situation like this. She began to cry. I was overwhelmed by a tangle of emotions, but the predominant one was fury, so that was the one I acted on. I demanded that she give the ring I'd bought her back. She handed it over and I walked away. I really loved her, but I had to pretend otherwise.

For about a month after that, my cousins and friends snickered and mocked me until I inwardly vowed never to be a sucker for love again. I felt betrayed in a way that I wasn't even able to recognize or describe; I had felt, if only briefly, that intimacy had allowed me to step into a more trusting, more protected world. Now there was nobody to confide in about how I felt. Who would understand? How had I not seen this betrayal coming? Did I cause this? I had been too young to become sexually involved; too many intense and mysterious emotions were attached to it that kept taking me over.

Soon, I moved from listening to R&B to rap songs in order to put my feelings about relationships and girls into some kind of context.

Rap elevated the guy, giving him control, while the woman was depicted as submissive. With most of us in households without father figures, we had no chance to see a humanized example of relationships; rap became our mythic illustration instead. Around that time, a group out of California called N.W.A. arrived with some real raw rap and an arsenal of songs and videos that captured the rising anger, the police brutality and racial profiling experienced by urban youth—along with their reputation for aggressively demeaning women. I soaked it all up. Everywhere around me in the neighborhood, I'd see guys reflecting the ill will so many of them had toward women as a result of recklessly scarred emotions. I felt an overwhelming flood of negative feelings toward intimate relationships with women after my experience with Kimberly. It put me on a path from there on out, one where I never fully committed to a relationship, and I kept going down that road for a long while.

3

DEVIANT, DELINQUENT, AND

DANGEROUS

In 1989, I had to switch schools again, this time to J.B. Hood Middle School. By then, I was coming to school with five and six thousand dollars tucked into my jeans pocket. I wore huge rope chain necklaces with a Nefertiti head hanging alongside crown-shaped medallions. My friends Bucky and Clay, cousins Rainbow and K-Ray, and me would roll up to school in rented limousines, rocking L.A. Gears and the latest Air Jordan warmup suits.

I tried to avoid all the drama and keep my grades up at J.B. Hood, but one afternoon I was sent to in-school suspension (ISS) for a minor infraction. There was another boy from a rival hood there with me. We started talking and got along pretty well, or so I thought. Later that night, though, one of my home girls called on three-way to say that the dude who'd been at ISS with me had said he wanted to slap me while hanging with me. *What the hell have I done to him?* I thought. Clearly, it didn't take much to provoke me: I told him he better meet me in the morning before school.

Word of our scheduled fight made it to school even before we did. When I arrived with my cousins, the rest of our neighborhood joined in behind us as we walked toward a crowd of about forty kids gathered in front. I came out from behind my cousins and called out to the guy who had said he was going to slap me. I'd spotted him ducking in the midst of his own crowd, looking like he was scared. His homies were staring at us hard; I could tell they wanted him to rep well for their hood. Then I heard someone shout, "Just shoot him! Just shoot him!" Out of nowhere, my homegirl Vee Walker stepped in front of me and said, ""Nah, you're gonna have to shoot me first." I heard a loud bang—and she was hit.

My mind slowed down even as the crowd started running and everybody started yelling. My cousins took off after the guy I'd come to meet and ended up fighting his homies. Vee was at my feet, squeezing my ankle. I leaned down and heard her murmur, "Damn, I'm shot." Her moans became louder until finally she said, "I don't want to die, Kiddo." I felt paralyzed standing over her body; a rage I'd never felt before overtook me. I told her it was going to be okay and put my hand on her abdomen, where blood was pouring out. And I stayed that way, blood dripping down my hand and arm, until the ambulance came.

Later that night, we found out that Vee was going to pull through. I was already plotting with my cousins to get revenge on the guy who'd shot her. Since the third grade, I'd been fighting—attacking someone or being attacked—but seeing someone else take a bullet for me had brought it to a new level. The image of Vee's gaze, the force of it diminishing as the blood poured out of her, held my brain captive all night.

The next day at school, the school principal called me to the office to suspend me, stating he had ample evidence that I was the actual target of the shooting and that I was creating an unsafe school environment. When my mother found out I had been the target of a shooting *and* suspended from school, it sent her into an emotional tailspin. She hardly talked to me during that time. When she looked at me, I couldn't tell if she wanted to cry or beat me.

But my life just kept veering farther off course. Soon after Vee was shot, my closest cousin K-Ray—the one I'd shared clothes with when we were younger—was arrested for murder, attempted murder, and aggravated robbery. Some older guys had put him up to robbing a couple of guys during a drug deal; things got rough, and K-Ray shot them. He was fifteen years old at the time of his arrest, but he turned sixteen while he was in juvenile and was then certified as an adult, which meant he was transferred to the county jail with grown men. He got fifteen years and ended up serving ten. His arrest should have spurred me to change, but I had developed a grandiose view of my role as a protector of East Dallas; I saw it as my obligation to step up and fill his shoes.

With K-Ray on lock, I found new friends to hang out with. They were all older than me, but they respected me for my hustle. One night, three days after K-Ray was arrested for murder, when I was nearly fourteen years old, they invited me to go to the Warehouse Club, a new nightspot in South Dallas. My friend KeeKee picked me up in his brother Tiger's lime green Z28 Camaro with the centerline 928 wheels and four fifteen-inch Cerwin-Vega woofers. We rode around the hood for a few minutes, showing off, then went to meet the rest of the crew, who joined us in a procession of cars pulling out of the projects at the same time. I still remember the feeling of pride I felt riding in the front seat of the car with the bass thumping, everybody waving at us and seeing me head out to the club for the first time.

This particular club sat directly under an overpass in a secluded area off Lamar Street in South Dallas. The music inside, "Ice Ice Baby" by Vanilla Ice, could be heard clear out onto the streets. Our crew was five cars deep in the parking lot. One of our homies, Chubby, had a Nissan truck with a red and purple camper. As soon as he parked his truck, the security guard came over and asked him to park somewhere else. While Chubby and the attendant were talking, I got out of the Z28 and checked my outfit to make sure I was tight; KeeKee and I had dressed alike in gold shirts and black shorts. I made a mental note not to smile so much, because that would be a dead giveaway of my age, to just stand back and watch everything.

As KeeKee and I were walking toward the club, we heard an argument start up between Chubby and the security guard. Out of respect for our homies, we walked back to see what was going on. But I was thinking to myself, "Yo, just move the truck so we can have a good time." Instead, the argument escalated. Chubby wasn't moving his truck and the security guard wasn't backing down. Suddenly, the security guard pulled out a big black police flashlight and hit Chubby over the head. Chubby, a big brawler, began to yell, and we all began to run.

As soon as we made it back to the Z28, we heard rapid gunfire. Everybody started trying to flee the parking lot. We were among the first cars out, but within minutes the police had surrounded us. They pulled out their guns, pointing them at us, and made us lay face down in a convenience store parking lot. Maybe I was in shock, maybe I didn't understand quite how serious the situation was, but I found myself worrying about ruining my outfit by lying in the grease and skid marks in the parking lot. I kept thinking about how impossible it would be for us to go back to the club with our outfits all messed up.

After about ten minutes, the police asked which one of us had been driving the truck. I didn't say anything; I didn't even look up. Suddenly, one of the policemen came over and picked me up by my arm and the back of the shirt and led me to the squad car. My heart started jumping. My mother's face popped into my mind; I couldn't imagine what she was going to say about this. "Wait, Officer, Officer . . . What am I being arrested for?" I asked.

"Because we found the gun in your truck," he replied.

I began to yell, "Sir, I don't have a truck, a license, or a gun. I'm only thirteen!"

They took me into juvie. The intake officer shook his head when he saw my name and said, "Another Lucky." I was led down a long hallway with steel doors and small enclosures that I assumed were for sliding in food or mail. The place smelled like a gymnasium. The other kids were beating on the doors, screaming and yelling obscenities as we passed. I was placed in a room and given a white jumpsuit and shower shoes to wear. One by one, the officer assigned each of us to pods and issued each of us a flat, light blue mattress. A younger officer with thick glasses and a fuzzy mustache led me to a tiny single cell. I threw my mattress over my shoulder and entered. I lay down, trying to be nonchalant and cool, but I was feeling more and more scared of how my life was spiraling out of control. Not far from my mind was Vee getting shot in the attempt made on my life at school, and now I had an unlawfully carrying a weapon charge at thirteen years old. As it turned out, one of the older guys we'd been with at the club had pointed the finger at me because he knew I was the youngest among us and I'd be let off easy with juvie. As it turned out, he was right: I was released the next day, with the expectation that I would attend a first offenders' program two months shy of my fourteenth birthday.

4

The Mouth of the Beast

By the summer of 1991, I'd been in and out of juvey three times. I was selling drugs for the Charles Ray organization, which was the biggest crack cocaine distributing operation in Dallas. Procaine was a thing of the past; people started realizing they were buying fake crack cocaine. I was now selling the real thing, and I was pulling in real cash. According to the FBI, the Charles Ray organization made about $1.5 million a week at that time. I never found out if that was actually true. What I do know was that, by that point, our operation at the carwash had started making forty thousand, at least, a day.

And I had become a gun-toting, crack-selling fourteen-year-old. By that time, making money had fully replaced my one-time aspiration of earning good grades; gangsters, pimps, and gang leaders had become pseudofather figures to me; sex had replaced my grandmother's hugs and kisses; learning how to use a gun had become essential to my continued existence.

There was no limit to the low and degrading things that addicts would do for crack. This was true even with some of my friends' parents—who were selling off everything they had, one by one, in order to buy just another hit of crack. Moms and dads I used to know as authority figures, or at least responsible adults, were now crawling, manipulating, pleading with me for more drugs. While I was in the midst of a deal, I put on a hard front; I was serious and rather blunt. But as soon as I left, I felt like I was going to fall to my knees, as if someone had knocked the wind out of me. Sometimes the urge to bless someone, like offer free money or help a stranger, would come over me. I hoped to balance out my bad deeds with good ones.

Several weeks later—the night before my first day of high school, actually—I was returning from a basketball game with my cousins and some other hustling partners from East Dallas. We'd been in Oak Cliff Sprague stadium, just south of Frazier Courts. We were rolling with a group of about eight cars and were less than two miles away from home when one the tires of my friend's car came off in Park Row. Park Row was officially Crips territory. The Crips are one of the largest, most violent street gangs in the U.S.—and they had a stranglehold on that part of the city. Even though Park Row and Frazier Courts, referred to as South and East Dallas, respectively, are basically in the same general area of Dallas, the rift between the Crips and our guys in East Dallas—better known as EDP, for East Dallas Projects—had created an invisible, barbed boundary between the two territories. As we waited for a tow truck, we all joked about what would happen if our rivals caught us over here. Everyone was laughing raucously, but when the tow truck finally arrived, I sensed a collective sigh of relief.

Only moments after the car was hooked up to the tow truck, though, gunshots rang out. We all hit the ground. As a spray of bullets rained down on us, I crawled under my car to escape. I looked in the direction of where the bullets were coming from and saw somebody standing behind a tree firing a shotgun and another figure next to him with a handgun; they had blue rags on their faces. We all managed to pile into our cars and speed back to Frazier Courts. Three of my friends had been hit with buck shot, but nobody was seriously hurt. We called some of our other homies, describing the shooters and their blue rags, making it known that they were Crips; we decided to wait on retaliation until the right time. In less than eight hours, I was going to arrive for my first day at Madison High School. It was not an auspicious way to start the year.

The next morning, all eyes were on me from the moment I pulled into the parking lot. I cruised around for a minute and then parked in a spot near the main entrance to the school. As I walked in, girls were smiling. At least seven dudes I didn't even know were mean-mugging me. I walked to the spot where I'd agreed to meet my friends. After dabbing and greeting my boys, I noticed all the people were separated into different hoods and thought to myself, *Man, ain't nothing changed since the fourth grade at Edna Rowe.* As we were all joking around, waiting for the bell to ring, a man with an authoritative walk strode up to our group, followed by the school police officer. He looked straight at me and shouted, "Kiddo, a.k.a. Antong Lucky?"

I had never heard an adult call me by my street name. I reluctantly nodded in acknowledgment. The man smirked and, pointing at each one of us, said in a smug tone, "You and Herbert Rider, a.k.a. Clay, Ronnie Walker, a.k.a. Tiger, Kelvin Walker, a.k.a. KeeKee—follow me."

As we followed him through the hall to his office, my swagger from just fifteen minutes earlier disappeared. We walked single file line behind the man, our heads bowed. I felt the eyes of other students burning into me as we walked shamefully along. Once we made it to his office, he turned around and introduced himself as Mr. Jones, the principal of James Madison. "I know who you are," he said, looking me in the eye, "and I am telling you straight to your face that if there are any problems out of any of you, you will all be suspended for the entire school year. I got word of who you are, and I know that you're running all the drugs and crime in the neighborhood." I tried to smile. On some level, I only ever really thought of myself as this good kid who just had a bad reputation. The principal shook his head.

That afternoon, my friends and I had made a plan to arrive in the parking lot immediately after the bell rang so we could show off our rides while school was coming to a close. Instead, when we got there, we found a large group of guys—all in blue bandanas—standing across the street at Angelo's supermarket. We instinctively ducked our heads and dispersed, each of us just trying to get to our cars and escape, but the Crips began firing before we had a chance. School buses were just pulling up; students were spilling out of the school building. Suddenly it was pure chaos. Kids started running in all different directions and screaming. I finally made it into my car. I was inching along, trying not to hit anyone as they scattered across the parking lot. I knew the Crips had me in their sights so when I finally made it out of the parking lot, I put my foot on the gas. Looking in my rearview mirror, I saw five guys with blue bandanas standing in the middle of the street, shooting in my direction. I realized that my high school career had just begun and ended on the same day.

The next morning, Mr. Jones was waiting for me in the parking lot when I drove into school. He led me to his office and told me that I was suspended for the rest of the year. He gave me a slip of paper, referring me to H.B. Bell and Dr. Alan Sullivan, the principals of an alternative school that he said I was now supposed to attend. As I walked out of his office, I threw the paper away and decided to spend the rest of my day at the carwash. Any last corner of hope in myself that I might get out of the game through some feat of capability or intuition was now boarded up. I was finished.

For the next week, I hustled all day and thought about how I was going to retaliate against the Park Row Crips for attacking us and getting me kicked out of school. But over the next few months, I settled into the job and set up more of an official operation to keep things running smoothly. I was the dealer, another guy took care of the money, and another served as a full-time look out for the police. One afternoon, I left the car wash on my bike—I was making most of my deliveries that way by then—and I passed by a police van going in the opposite direction. I stopped my bike and looked back toward the car wash. I saw the van pull in—I believe my heart stopped beating for a moment—and then many officers jumped out. It was a raid. I saw them grab my cousin Rainbow—who'd only just gotten out of juvie—and, without even thinking about it, I jumped back on my bike. I started pedaling furiously back toward Rainbow. I didn't have a plan; I just knew I couldn't let my cousin go back to juvie, or worse, without trying to intervene. I suppose I thought I might be able to talk our way out of this. As I was racing down the street, another police van pulled in front of me, the door slid open, and a pile of officers jumped out and grabbed me. "We got him! We got him!" the officers yelled to their colleagues at the car wash as they threw handcuffs on me and pressed my head down to get me into the back of the van. As it turned out, it had been a sting operation—I'd sold to an undercover cop earlier in the day. They arrested me for delivery of a controlled substance. But at least Rainbow went free.

The police told me they'd been hearing my name in too many

places, and I was likely headed to TYC—the Texas Youth Commission. TYC was prison for kids under the age of eighteen, the place that Rainbow had just been released from. The Crip gang basically ran it. I'd heard cruel stories from Rainbow of dudes from East Dallas getting harassed and gang-jumped daily. Even though our neighborhood wasn't yet gang affiliated, the Crips hated us. I was terrified to go—the cops had said it would probably be for three years—but if it was to be, then I would be ready to face it.

Instead, two months later, my probation officer told me that I was being given the option to go to a place called Glen Mills State School. He said this would be the better option over TYC—Glen Mills was a well-known institution, the oldest reform school for boys in the U.S. In fact, he acted as if I'd won the lottery—as if I were actually lucky to be able to attend this mystery school just outside of Philadelphia, PA—and my mother was in agreement. I didn't want to go out of state, but I knew it *had* to be better than fighting every day at the Texas Youth Commission.

On June 3, 1992, I boarded the first plane I'd ever been on and considered all that had happened until that point. I thought about how I had been expelled from school every year since the seventh grade. I thought about all the fights, the close calls with guns, and how Vee had nearly died for me. I thought about the car wash and the money I'd stashed and the Cadillac that I had left with a friend. I thought about how my grandmother had passed away not long before—taking with her the last bastion of stability in our family. Lastly, I thought about my mother sitting next to me in the courtroom and the pained look on her face when the judge bellowed out that I would be leaving home for the next three years.

5

How Do You Behave?

When I arrived at the airport in Philadelphia, I spotted two enormous white men—they looked as if they were body-builders, with biceps the size of footballs—wearing Glen Mills T-shirts. I walked over to them; there was a short introduction of names, followed by awkward smiles and full up-and-down body stares from both of them. I assumed they were admiring my outfit—I was wearing my black leather jacket, designer shades, and Jordans. I had no idea where to get my suitcases, as I'd never flown before, so I asked, "Where are my bags?" One of the guys replied, "Would you like me to get them for you?" I said yes and thanked him. Suddenly, out of nowhere, in the middle of the airport, he jacked me up by my collar and said, "I don't know who you think you are son, but I'll kick your ass!" I was stunned and embarrassed by this explosion and had no idea what this guy was trying to prove. I shook him off and then reluctantly followed the men as they turned on their heels and walked away.

As it turned out, they were picking up two other arrivals—and then they picked up our bags too, after all. The two other students seemed as bewildered as I was as these strange dudes silently led us single file through the airport and into the parking lot. Finally, we reached the car, and the three of us piled into the backseat while the two body builders sat upfront. I was still upset, trying to process what had happened at the airport.

At one point, when the car drove through what appeared to be a middle-class neighborhood and turned under a bridge, some little white kids threw rocks at the car. I could tell that it startled the guards. The other two kids in the back with me laughed—which caused one of the men to turn around toward the backseat and say, "Oh, you think that's funny? We're going to show you what's funny when we get to the school, motherfucker." He said it to all of us, but he was looking dead at me.

True to their word, when we arrived at Glen Mills, I was taken into a small office in an administrative building, where about five other guys that looked like clones of the first two guards from the airport crowded in. Later, I learned that most of the staff were military retirees and power lifters. These guys started winding me up—"You got a problem? You think you know better than anyone, motherfucker?" And started closing in on me in a circle. Then they started pushing me, until finally I couldn't hold back anymore, and I lunged back at one of them. I didn't stand a chance; I was a 145-pound sixteen-year-old going up against these thugs. The next thing I knew, I was flying up against a stack of desks stored in the corner of the room. I remember hitting the ground, in searing pain, and thinking, *Man, this is real.* I couldn't believe this was happening at what my probation officer had touted as "the greatest reform school in the country," as if he were doing me a favor. I was two thousand miles from home; there was nowhere to run.

Glenn Mills was an immaculately kept facility founded in 1826.

People considered it a kind of Ivy League of juvenile detention centers—and it looked the part too. The school was comprised of elegant redbrick buildings sitting amidst an obsessively manicured eight-hundred-acre campus, with meadows and streams, along with its own eighteen-hole golf course next door. Kids were sent from all over the country—California, New York, Ohio, and, of course, Texas—and though it was a privately run nonprofit, the taxpayers mostly paid our lofty tuitions.

First and foremost, we were taught to be "civil" to one another. When we passed by one another in the hallway, we were told to ask, "How do you behave?" If we passed a staff member we were required to say, "Good morning, sir" or "ma'am," whatever the case might be. Glen Mills also had a "system" to help students stay in line. For this, we were made the monitors of our peers' behavior. If a student observed another kid doing something wrong, he could ask for support from his peers to confront the person and make them aware of their wrongful ways. If that didn't work, they could call in staff for support; this usually resulted in an action known as "touched for attention." It sounds either innocent or sexually sordid, depending on your character and experience, I guess; in reality, though, the phrase signaled that the counselors were now free to bust your lip or knock you unconscious or slam you into a wall—which they once did to me so forcefully the wall burst open.

Needless to say, I didn't like that system.

The school also rated all its students on their behavior: positive bull, neutral bull, negative bull, and major concern; these were largely based on the school mascot, a battling bull. From the start, I was classified as a major concern. As a result, everywhere I went, I had to be accompanied by one of the menacing staff members.

Positive bulls were the leaders of the group. These students had accepted—and were excelling in—the system; they were doing all the right things, we were told, to go home and become productive citizens. What this actually meant was that those kids were being herded like terrified sheep, reporting other students to staff every time they saw negative behavior, ultimately resulting in those kids being beaten. Those considered *neutral* were barely skating by and needed to step up in order to consider being able to go home with a good rating. The *negative* classification was reserved for those who needed to climb up from the bottom. *Major concern* basically meant you were a lost cause, with permanent permission granted to the staff to let loose on you. The school also held regular Town Halls, when the whole dorm gathered to hear staff rules or to listen to a punishment that was being handed out; this was also the time at which students were brought up for "feedback," at which point all the other students were allowed to yell out all the terrible things they'd seen that particular kid do.

During one of these Town Halls, the only other kid from Texas had to "bring himself up" for feedback; he stood in front of the whole school and explained why he was being disciplined. Then all the other students rushed in at him, until they were just inches from his face, yelling negative comments about his behavior, while he stood motionless. If you were at the center of this commotion, you were not allowed to flinch or move. The staff members cheered the angry mob of students on. They even allowed those kids to haul off and spit all over the guy's face. He stood with their saliva dripping down his face, hardly blinking and completely silent. It was a horrifying exercise in humiliation and contempt.

The next day, I privately told the kids who'd participated in that heinous exercise that I would happily risk being *touched for attention* before I would allow anyone to treat me like that. "If I have to bring myself up at Town Hall," I told them, "and you so much as come near me, I'm going to knock you out." My message was clear: do not disrespect me. And since the staff was beating me regularly and I hadn't cracked under that kind of pressure, they heard it.

Sure enough, soon after I had to ask for feedback over something petty that had happened in class. I found myself at a Town Hall, surrounded by sixty-four of my peers, reluctantly announcing, "My name is Antong Lucky, and I would like to bring myself up." Because the staff thought I was being too cocky, I was asked to reintroduce myself three more times. Hands began to go up all over the room. The staff eagerly yelled out for feedback. The first person said, "Lucky, man, what I got for you is to just chill." A staff member called on the next person and he said, "Lucky, you're doing a good job." Visibly frustrated, the staff yelled "Feedback" over and over; each student showed restraint and respect in his remarks. Finally, in a wild rage, one of the counselors said, "Since y'all act like you're so afraid of Lucky, get all y'all asses on the floor, and Lucky, sit your ass on the couch." I'd always sat on the floor with the other negative bulls at Town Hall meetings. That night, though, in his fury, the counselor bafflingly granted me a positive rating while downgrading everyone else to a negative. Oddly, after that, the staff members had a grudging admiration for me; they treated me more as one of them, as if I had come up through their contorted ranks by beating my fellow students into submission.

Glen Mills was also well known for its athletics, with state-of-the-art facilities and stadiums and a demanding athletics programs that yielded top prizes and NFL recruits. I didn't play a particular

sport, so when the track coach, Rich, recruited me for his team, sug-
gesting that I come to one practice and see how I liked it, I agreed.
I didn't much care for it at the first practice though, so I told Rich
I wasn't interested. "Sorry to hear that because you're now on the
team," he replied and walked away. Again, I felt played. The spirit of
rebellion rose inside of me, but I was able to restrain it.

It was the one act of disregard at Glen Mills that actually had
a positive impact on me. I started running five to ten miles a day. I
found that I was able to clear my mind with long-distance running—
forgetting the threatening atmosphere of the school and the alien-
ated feeling of being suddenly thrust into this complicated system,
which now felt as far away as the moon. I became one of the top run-
ners at the school; Coach Rich started challenging those who wanted
to join the track team to try to keep up with me in order to see if
they had the stamina to continue. Running was about escape and
survival, but it also became a source of pride. It allowed me to leave
Glen Mills with at least a small glimmer of positive feeling, though
still conflicted with the process.

Over the years, I allowed this glimmer to push out the hostile
mood that I felt more generally about my experience at the school.
Mostly, I tried to forget about it and move on. But twenty-six years
after I'd graduated, I met a guy in Dallas who worked in the juvenile
department and was a recruiter for Glen Mills; I told him about my
experience and asked him directly if such things were still happening. He shook his head. "It's not like that now," he said.

Soon after, he connected me with the school to speak to the student body as a celebrated alumnus. It was a strange experience, to put
it mildly, walking the campus as an adult. I saw my photograph hung
on the "wall of fame." I spoke to some of the students, giving them

inspirational life lessons, also trying to discern if the same abuse was still occurring. At one point, walking down a hallway near where the infamous Town Halls had taken place—wincing at the memory of both the shame brought on the students and my own bullying efforts to protect myself—I ran into a teacher from my days there who was still on staff. When we caught eyes, he seemed braced for confrontation; his body hummed with anticipation as I approached.

There was a bit of small talk and then a pause. "I'm past what happened here. I forgive you," I said. "I'm blessed now and doing a lot of good things. So we're alright." He knew what I meant. The counselor, now in his sixties, sighed. "I appreciate it, Lucky," he said. I didn't ask him point blank if he still felt free to hit the students— perhaps I wasn't ready to hear it. At any rate, I forgave the bully who busted my lip at sixteen years old, so I guess time does heal all wounds. In any case, I left, somehow reassured that the abusive culture of the school had shifted.

About a year after my return visit, however, I received an email about a class action lawsuit, following an investigation by the *Philadelphia Inquirer*, which was being filed by current and former students against Glen Mills and the staff who'd assaulted and abused them. My heart sank. Stories poured forth about boys being chopped in the throat, kicked, slammed, and punched; one boy had been so badly beaten that, as one counselor described it, his eye had been nearly knocked out of its socket. The school has since had its licenses revoked by the Pennsylvania Department of Human Services and is currently being investigated by the U.S. Department of Justice. In response, Glen Mills has denied allegations of mistreatment and appealed to have its licenses restored. It forced me to pry open the tidier narrative I'd created about the school for myself—about my time there *and* in recognition of the kids who were still suffering even as I had walked the corridors just a year before. I thought about the sixteen-year-old boy—and the thousands of kids just like him— who'd arrived there looking for an escape from the trouble he'd found at home, only to find a place that seemed to promise there was *no* safe corner in the world at all.

6

———◆———

LOSING ME

March 22, 1993: on the plane ride back from Pennsylvania to Dallas, I planned to lead a completely different lifestyle. I had decided to go back to Madison High School, run track, and get my high school diploma. When I arrived at home, my mother and brothers made me feel as if I were returning from the marines or something—they were shocked by how much I'd grown and the size of my muscles. Despite the steep challenges of Glen Mills, eating well, running, and going to bed early had thoroughly and positively changed how I looked.

In my mind, I was reconnecting, but the impression I was giving to my friends and family was that I was stepping back into life just as I had left it. Whether I knew it then or not, I was back in the game.

One night, not long after I'd returned, I was standing with some friends in "the hole"—an area between apartment complexes in the projects not accessible from the street known as a place protected from drive-bys. As we talked, a woman pulled into the parking lot with her two young kids. She parked the car and ran into her apartment to grab something, leaving her kids waiting in the back seat of the car. Out of nowhere, two huge dudes walked up. Standing less than a hundred feet from us, they pulled out AK-47s and start blasting down into the hole. I jumped up and dove under the woman's car, shouting at the kids to get down. Their frantic screams echoed across the projects. Bullets riddled the car; glass flew everywhere. Concrete popped off the sides of the apartment building. Then, as quickly as it had started, it stopped. The only sounds left were the fierce cries of the children and their terrified mother calling for them.

I rolled out from under the car with blood all over me. I didn't know whether I was hit or not; my first concern was the children. I opened the car door and saw blood pouring down the little boy's arm. I felt my legs go watery beneath me. Just looking at the river of blood was completely unnerving. During the shooting, the little boy, who couldn't have been more than seven years old, had covered the girl with his body to protect her. His finger had been shot off. But otherwise, astonishingly, he was fine. The flying glass had cut me in several places, though I was also not seriously harmed. That experience, however, withered any last ambition I had to try to live life on the straight and narrow.

Later that night, we found out that the murderous attempt had been a walk-by commissioned by the Crip gang. My cousins and I, along with a few neighborhood friends, decided that we needed to form more of an official alliance—a united front—to defend ourselves against the ceaseless attacks on East Dallas. We knew that the fights we'd been having over the years were all with the Crip gang; they'd always faithfully worn their blue bandanas to be sure we got that message. So the next day we went to the Bazaar and bought red bandanas and hats and declared ourselves Bloods. We spread the word, adopting "415" as our set and distinguishing us as the only

Bloods in Dallas at that time. We realized we had to be the deadliest, most ruthless neighborhood. Pretty soon, the whole neighborhood was dressing in red bandanas, Dickies, and Chuck Taylors; we modeled ourselves after the Piru Street Boys and Westside Piru gangs, the original Bloods from Compton, California. We even changed our language, creating a new vernacular, replacing C with B, so as never to even come near uttering the letter that started our rival's name. "Kicking back, being cool," for instance, became "Bicking back, being bool." It was excessive, but we knew that we were outnumbered so everything we did had to be bigger. It was a new beginning for our neighborhood, and the pronouncement of war. That year—1994— became the deadliest one on record for gang violence in Dallas, Texas.

The transformative mindset I'd had leaving Glen Mills didn't last ninety days. I went back to hustling at the car wash. I spent my nights working there and tried to go to school during the days. Some of my friends tried to convince me to drop out so I wouldn't be an open target, but graduating school was a finishing line I was still desperately trying to cross. Until, that is, the Park Row Crips finally did come back around for me. One afternoon, as I walked out into the school parking lot, I found more than fifty Crips across the streets hurling gang signs at me. It was reminiscent of my first day of school there.

The principal came running out, along with the school police, and warned me not to go across the street, but I knew I couldn't look or act fearful, so I stepped to the curb, and I began to throw gang signs back at them. I'd figured they wouldn't dare cross the street with the police present—but suddenly car horns started blaring and they all started running toward me. Pretty soon, I was on the ground, getting kicked and stomped all over my body. Seconds later, I saw the principal go down next to me and they were jumping him too. I remember the almost sweet feeling of my consciousness leaving when I heard a round of gunshots. There were too many to count, especially in my dazed state, but they brought my free-for-all beating to a sudden end.

As I opened my eyes, looking out ahead of me, I saw my homies in a line of cars at least seven deep. I heard Piru Love pumping out of the speakers. They'd cleared everyone out. Barely able to walk and completely covered in blood, I stumbled over to the closest car. I looked back at the principal, who was still down but moving, and then fell into the car. As we sped off, I knew that I wouldn't be coming back; that was the end of my high school education.

Drive-bys and shootouts became a regular way of life. Our hood was ours to bleed; we could sell as much drugs as our community could buy and no one else could come anywhere near our turf—but we also weren't foolish enough to try selling anywhere else. Over the course of the next few years, East Dallas came to resemble modern-day Iraq or Aleppo. The houses and businesses were peppered with bullet holes and covered in gang graffiti. During that time, it was better to be caught with a gun than without one; a single sloppy move could cost you your life.

And my name was ringing among the police because my drug-selling game had started to take off once more. I was a target and I knew it, so I paid extra attention to small details all the time. But I also felt cocky about my survival skills; I'd already come through far more than what had taken so many other homies out. I felt compelled to be "OG Kiddo," the neighborhood representative, but at the same time I was losing myself to what the hood said I had to be. This was the life that the streets had given me, though, and I was determined to figure it out.

7

COPS AND CRACK HOUSES

The years of constant gang banging became the most depressing time of my life. Every day, someone from the original Frazier Court gang fell victim to the Crips, the cops, or the cemetery. We lived every day wondering if it would be our last. I was bitterly unhappy, I felt it deep in my bones, but I didn't have the strength, or option, to walk away. Just like the crack smokers who couldn't stop their daily ritual of addiction, I awoke every morning and staggered through a day of violence.

Each morning began, for me, around 11:00 a.m. My first stop after leaving my apartment in Frazier Courts was the basketball court to oversee a new gang initiation. A year had passed since we had founded the Bloods. By then, we had grown in notoriety and numbers despite the losses we were taking every day. And anyone who wanted to join us, had to go through our initiation to get their number five, which then certified them as a 415 member. To receive that coveted five, the new recruit had to stand toe to toe against five other Bloods in a circle and fight without folding.

As the person overseeing this process, I was the only one who could start or stop it. Very few could endure more than four minutes and fifteen seconds; I stopped the timer depending on the amount of blood flowing from the wannabe's face. If somebody got knocked out or stopped fighting, then they failed the initiation; if they continued to fight regardless of the pain and dizziness, we accepted them.

After initiation, I tried to be the first person to the car wash to make sales to the early-bird smokers. Getting started early was a necessity because standing on the corner slanging at nighttime had become increasingly dangerous, both because of drive-bys and the police. Slowly, too, the financial incentive of gang banging had been starting to erode. Many of the older gang members had naturally evolved out of the day-to-day activities associated with banging; they were opening crack houses instead as a way of selling in a crowded market. It seemed like I was one of the last few still hustling on my own—while also hiding out because of my oversized reputation.

Then, one morning in early March 1995, one of my friends informed me that the Feds had just left, banging on my door in East Dallas, arresting forty-eight people, all with sealed indictments. It was an apocalyptic event for those of us who only knew how to make living off the East Dallas underworld. It also felt like a small miracle that I hadn't been on their list; I thought perhaps it was actually because I'd kept business small, selling only part-time as of late. The other dealers were hauled off to the Seagoville federal detention center. Many of the huge personalities within our community were gone in an instant. Crack houses were immediately emptied, their doors swinging open. Cars were confiscated. And the demand for crack skyrocketed.

Seeing dealers, hustlers, and players busted had a chilling effect on me. Those were the dudes I'd grown up with; they were the ones who'd inducted me into the business, and they'd taught me the rules—the first among them being to remain loyal and don't snitch. Now word had it they were snitching on each other, trying to get the best plea deals possible. Some were even said to be willing to take the stand to rat their own brothers out. The more I heard, the less I felt like I was standing on solid ground. Nothing familiar remained.

My friend Clay and I called Amy and asked her if we could work at her mother's home health care business in the suburbs. Amy had just had a baby with Clay—and she wanted to help us out. So her mother, Mrs. Linda, decided to give us a job doing filing and clerical work. She hired us at minimum wage for six months, and I was able to get out of the hood every day, off everyone's radar.

Working for Mrs. Linda taught me to appreciate what my mother had done for so many years while supporting us and trying to keep us safe. I also felt good about doing some honest and legal work for once. It was a relief not to have to look over my shoulder or stay up at night watching my back. Mrs. Linda taught us how to file paperwork, keep track of accounts, and keep the office clean. Still, making the adjustment to legal money was tough to embrace. It provided the assurance that I wasn't going to jail, but it also felt entirely too slow for me. So as time went by and the FBI bust began to look more like a one-time thing, I felt the call of pharmaceutical entrepreneurship once more luring me back.

The game was starting back up again, and it was changing fast. Crack houses became where the addicts simply did drugs, whereas "traps" became the place where product was purchased. This new era brought forth a different type of hustler. Trap houses were the responsibility of particular dealers trying to make more money, and each one was run like a small business. Outperforming the competition became the name of the game. And to survive, you had to be respected in the hood—with a tightly run operation and fine product—so that the drug addicts didn't cross you out and gangs didn't jack you. You also had to be able to outthink the cops.

I had put a lot of thought into how I'd run my own traps while working for Mrs. Linda's home health care business. And once I'd managed to secure a few of my own, I ran them with strict metrics for turning a profit. I negotiated the best prices for my cocaine, buying low and selling high. I paid a lady to cook the cocaine into crack. I marketed my product by giving it to addicts for free to start, giving them a taste of how good it was so they'd keep coming back for more. And on every street where I had a trap, I rented another house on the other side of the street where my employees could chill and where crack was not allowed. That way, the police couldn't bust them. I had an ever-changing pick-up routine for the money. I rode my bicycle through the neighborhood, checking on the addicts, making sure they were happy with the quality of product that they wanted. I let them know not to bring me anyone they didn't know during hard times and they would have credit with me. This shielded me from possible undercover agents. Within months, financially, I was back to where I had left off before the FBI had cracked down; within two months, I was clearing about thirty-five hundred a day after payouts.

8

GOOD GIRLS

Although most of the others in my set also accessorized their dope boy lifestyle with a string of girlfriends, many of whom lived too close for comfort in the same part of the hood or apartment building in Frazier Courts, I was always drawn to the squeaky-clean girls on the outside. These girls were the valedictorians of their high schools, college-bound, decidedly *not* interested in dope boys.

My first girlfriend, when money was rolling and I was able to do as I pleased, had been a girl named Kesha. I'd actually met her through Amy, the mother of Clay's child. Kesha's father owned a gas station and a car lot and was also part owner of a funeral home. Kesha worked all three places, which kept her busy every day after school. She was a drama-free, positive person who dreamed of a better life for herself—at the same time, though, we had to keep our relationship on the down low, because the rivalry between the Bloods and the Crips had gotten so bad, gang members' girlfriends were being targeted. Because of this, our relationship was brief, never really having a chance to develop, despite how bonded I felt to her.

Not long after Kesha and I had drifted apart, on a hot summer weekend when I was nineteen years old, I pulled up to a red light in my homie's yellow Chevy 1500 truck with chrome Dayton wire wheels and a picture of the Dallas skyline painted on the back tailgate that lit up at night. I looked in my rearview mirror and saw a schoolmate of mine running up toward me. She told me that her cousin wanted to holler at me. "Where she at?" I asked and she pointed to a nearby car. Inside, I saw one of the most beautiful girls I'd ever seen. Kenyada was light-skinned, and she had a beauty mole on her lip. Her curvy shape told me that she was athletic; after talking to her for a bit, I learned that she was a cheerleader, a sweet country girl from Kansas.

For the rest of the summer, all I did was check my traps and spend time with Kenyada. We got along so well and it was so easy to spend time with her that I caught a glimpse of the feeling I'd had as a young kid, back when I fell in love for that first time with Kimberly. I felt both excited and vigilant. As much as I wanted to escape into our romance, I never again wanted to experience the anguish I'd felt when Kimberly betrayed me. Meanwhile, I always had to pick Kenyada up at night so as not to be noticed by the Crips or cops. Once, picking Kenyada up for a date, her mother asked me suspiciously, "Why do you always pick up my daughter up after dark?" I tried to laugh it off, wondering how I was going to continue to juggle my reckless lifestyle and my desire to connect with someone outside of it. That September, Kenyada went off to college. We were still very bound up in our relationship, so I promised to travel to see her on the weekends and to be a faithful friend and lover.

By winter, though, I'd met another girl, Deborah. I'd spotted her walking her dog while I was riding my bike, leaving one of my traps. I had never seen her before—and yet she seemed comfortable walking her dog down the street in my hood. I tried to speak to her then, riding slowly alongside her on my bike, but she gave me the cold shoulder. A few days later, I drove past her in one of my Cadillacs, and she turned her head the other way. I drove past her in a different car a few days later, and again she turned away. Finally, I asked one of my neighbors about her. He told me that she was over here visiting her father; she was a "church girl" who was enrolled in Paul Quinn College, and she definitely did not date hood, thug, gangbanging dudes like myself. Soon after, I also learned that she went to Griggs Chapel Baptist Church—and I went to a midweek service there myself, dressed in a black suit, a white silk shirt with a pair of black gators. When the Pastor gave the invitation to join the church, I took the long walk down the aisle.

Deborah was unlike any girl I'd ever met. She was beautiful, intelligent, inquisitive, and very nurturing. She wanted the best for me. She wanted me to go to college, to church, to hang around a better set of friends. She insisted on meeting my mother. She took me by storm.

But my world was torn in two when Kenyada returned from college. I'd managed to keep both relationships going—in part because I'd seen everyone else juggle more than one girlfriend at once but also because I was still holding part of myself back for fear of getting hurt. Truthfully, looking back over that stage of my life, I think I craved the admiration and love of those good girls because I had a desire for a life of family, respect, and honor—but I was also just hardened enough, and full of myself, to believe I didn't have to do the work to make that happen. Somehow, I believed that those women would confer their goodness on me—and I didn't consider making a choice between them as long as I could get away with it.

So I spent the summer seeing both of them. Kenyada was living at home—and there was no way her mother was going to let me spend the night. Deborah had her own apartment, and she allowed me to keep my own schedule given how busy things were in my work life. I even managed to keep a double life going with Kenyada about that; she had no idea that I was in a gang. It was thoughtless and unstable, but I was also furiously winging it. There was no rulebook or guide. I was hustling, trying to stay alive, oblivious as to how to form a healthy relationship. That fall, however, just before she was meant to go back to school, Kenyada told me that she was pregnant. And, suddenly, what had seemed mostly like play-acting took a heavy turn.

A month after that, I was arrested. I'd been out heading to Home Depot when one of my guys called to say that he was out of product. I had a system set up so that was never supposed to happen. There was a guy who sold at the trap and another guy who made sure he was always supplied with product and who picked up the drug money, as well as delivered payroll weekly. But on that particular day, the guy with the drugs was nowhere to be found. So I said I'd swing by, pick up the money, and try to figure out what was going on. When I arrived, though, even before I'd entered the house, a police van pulled up. Immediately, I lay down in the driveway. My dealer, who'd come out to greet me, went face down about twenty feet from me. The police were wearing black ski masks; they were undercover narcotics officers, so they were meant to keep their identities protected. I held out hope that since my dealer was out of crack—and we weren't at the house where the drug deals took place—we'd be okay. But when they turned my dealer over on his back and searched him, they found a Crown Royal bag filled with several ounces of cocaine—I later learned that was his personal stash—along with five thousand in cash. "That's mine," the dealer said to the smirking cops as soon as they lifted the bag of drugs and money.

"Nah, I saw Lucky throw it," one of the officers said, a cop I thought I recognized from his eyes and build. He'd always threatened he was going to get me one day.

"You're a liar!" I shouted.

"It's mine, I swear it's mine," the dealer pleaded.

The police went into a huddle just a few feet away from me. I heard the officer say again that he'd seen me throw the bag. Since I didn't actually physically sell drugs anymore, that was the only way he was going to get me.

The police charged both of us, me and my dealer. I bonded out on bail, hired a lawyer, and got the dealer to sign an affidavit that the drugs had been his own personal property in his possession.

While waiting for my court date, I began going to the courtroom every day to observe the other cases. I wanted to study how I could best build my case, how I could prove that the officer who had charged me had also framed me. Kenyada was pregnant, and if I couldn't prove that those drugs weren't mine I was going to jail. It felt like my life had suddenly sped off without me and I was sprinting, out of breath, just trying to keep up.

I began to observe a dismally reliable pattern in these courtroom dramas: a Black kid was charged, a white expert was brought in to explain how the drug world worked, an all-white jury listened and deliberated, and, more often than not, day in, day out, they passed down a guilty verdict.

What was different for me, my attorney insisted, was that I had a signed affidavit from my dealer who was willing to admit that the drugs were his own. On the other hand, what I had going against me were four veteran narcotics officers willing to boldly lie under oath, alleging that they saw me throw the bag.

On the day of my trial, as we stood outside the court room waiting to go in, another young Black guy, a friend of mine, was being tried. Suddenly, I heard a piercing wail and then hollering and crying; my friend's family came bursting out the courtroom doors, his mother bent over, weeping. I asked one of his brothers what had happened. "They just gave him twenty years," he said somberly and then pushed past me. I turned to my lawyer, looking for more of the encouragement he'd been giving me up to that point—some sense that my story would be different; we had an affidavit. I'd be okay.

"How do you feel about us?" I asked.

"Lucky, man, we can go in there and try," he said, shaking his head, looking as if we'd already been handed a guilty verdict. "You're in an unfavorable position with drug selling and, more than likely, you're going to have a white DA, a white judge, and an all-white jury that is not going to be able to relate to you."

It seemed as if he'd turned into someone else with entirely different advice than he'd been giving me all along. My heart felt like it was scrambling up the side of my body. I couldn't go to jail. I hadn't committed the crime!

I asked if we could get probation. The lawyer suggested that he go back with an open plea—meaning I would have to plead guilty but there would be a possibility of me not receiving a sentence. Instead, the judge allowed us to postpone for a week; we were instructed to come back with character witnesses. We'd bought ourselves some more time, and I was plunged back into a sea of uncertainty.

9

THE BEAST

As I stood in the courtroom, having heard the positive testimony of seven of my character witnesses, I felt hopeful. This was my first felony offense, and my lawyer, returning to his earlier optimism, had advised me that this likely meant I'd get probation. I imagined how many people such as myself pleaded guilty for something they didn't do, at the advice of their lawyer. Just two weeks before, Kenyada had given birth to our baby girl—Tileyah—and something had broken open in me. I had been terrified when I got the call that Kenyada was in labor. In fact, I'd felt so overwhelmed I hadn't immediately rushed to the hospital. I suppose I was embarrassed at how empty-handed I'd felt when the call came. What was I supposed to do? How on earth was I supposed to act? I am sorry to say I didn't actually go to the hospital until the day after our baby daughter was born. When I arrived, Kenyada was upset and wanted to know where I'd been—and I'd lied, too easily, about having to do something for work—but when I held our baby for the first time, I'd felt a surge of love and faith that I wouldn't go to jail. I *couldn't* be taken away from being a father.

"You are a menace to society," the judge said to me.

The response in my head went like this: *But wait, Judge—that's not me. I was only pretending so I can survive in my neighborhood.* But the words never came out of my mouth.

I was sentenced to seven years in the Texas Department of Criminal Justice. I was instantly separated from my daughter, and the world as I knew it. Instead, I was repeating a history I'd sworn I'd never repeat. How had this happened? I'd been moving so fast I hadn't even recognized the shadow—looming always ahead—that I'd stepped into. *I am my father,* I realized as soon as the judge sentenced me. I felt a hot rush of anger. My father, or rather his absence, had been such a heavy burden. If I had been able to see the way my own life was taking shape—of how readily I had allowed my father's fate to dictate my own—I like to think I would have struggled mightily against it. But as it was, my eyes had not been opened until too late. My deepest fear—though I had yet to articulate it to myself—was that I'd be swallowed by the beast; I would become irrelevant and forgotten or, worse, a memory of someone you hope *not* to be like, as my own father had been to me. My introspection began as I started thinking about how the system played me.

When I arrived at the back gates of prison, after staying in Dallas County jail for just over a month, I was hustled in the back door of a tin building where there was a line of small cages—these were our holding cells. The officer's tone, as he herded us into them, was a bit over the top, as if he were going to lose it at any moment. I kept thinking, *Why does the officer have so much animosity toward us?* But everyone else seemed to take it in stride, so I just kept moving along. He ordered everyone to strip naked. Then we were asked to step out and line up. I assumed we would be handed new clothes. Instead, we

all stood there in line, buck naked, shifting our weight, casually drop-
ping our hands to cover our privates. After a few minutes, several
other correctional officers came in, and the one who'd been giving out
instructions previously began to show off for his friends; he started
barking at us even louder. His excitement seemed to be chaotically
spiraling upward as the officers observed us all lined up, without the
defense of clothing, looking like something out of a slave auction
story. "Bend over," the officer ordered, "and spread your cheeks."

At first, I thought I'd heard him wrong. But as the others were
already complying, I realized that was not the case. My eyes darted
down the line; I wanted to find just one other person looking like
I was feeling. Was there no way out of this? Within minutes, the
officer was in front of me. I was still struggling with the command—
something deep inside told me to get it over with already. So I turned
as quickly as I possibly could and bent over. But when I whipped
around to face the officer again, he was shaking his head as if something wasn't right. He said I hadn't shown him the bottom of my feet.
So, reluctantly, I turned again and put one foot up, then the next, as
he checked to be sure I hadn't managed to smuggle anything into
prison on—or in—my body. It felt humiliating and degrading.

After getting our prison uniforms, a haircut, and the dreaded
institutional number, 788484, I was then sent to an interview with a
classification officer. The questions were simple and straightforward,
but they cut me like a knife.

"What type of work did you do in society?"

"Texas has no record of your GED from Glen Mills, so we consider you a high school dropout. Your juvenile record begins at the
age of thirteen and shows a continued disregard for the laws of the
State."

What could I say?

He recommended that I be given a job in the "Ho Squad," the nickname for the guys working in the fields with hoes.

The Hutchins Unit compound consisted of a series of dorms that housed inmates in double bunks. One side of the unit was for TDCJ inmates; the other side was for state jail inmates. A slab of concrete called the bowling alley connected the different buildings. The church, chow hall, education department, and infirmary were all tin warehouses converted into a building used for the purpose it was named for.

When I picked up my mattress to head to my assigned dorm, I noticed some homies throwing me gang signs—some from people I knew but too many from guys I'd never seen before. I began to see others being hit up by their Crip homies. While I most definitely wouldn't run from a fight or a clique, I was not expecting to come to prison to gangbang. I had made a decision while I was being held in county jail that I was going to make conscious changes in my behavior in order to get back to my daughter as soon as I could.

I walked into my dorm and threw my mattress on my bunk. Two bunks were stacked on top of each other; these were separated by about three feet of space from the next set of bunks. There was an open area where everyone sat to watch TV—this was the day room. Nothing stood between the day room and the showers. This, I would soon learn, would be my biggest psychological hurdle in prison. Every time I would peel off my clothes to take a shower, the female officers would look me dead in the eye; meanwhile, wide smiles would stretch across the faces of dudes who were clearly gay, who would just happen to be watching TV all day long. It was an impossible choice: I could either turn away, showing them my ass, or offer them a full-frontal view but hiding my ass. Either way, they enjoyed the show. This felt more brutal and invasive than any of the violent beat-downs that occurred behind bars; it was a sickening daily marker of how little was left of my privacy and how degraded my life had become.

On that first day, as I looked around, growing more and more enraged at the situation, the only area that didn't seem open for everyone to view was the corner of the room, largely obscured by one wall, where several people huddled, smoking cigarettes. A jumble of noise blared out: two blaring televisions, men slamming dominoes down, and younger men slap-boxing each other in what looked like a courage-building exercise. Moment by moment, my anxiety mounted.

I jumped up on my top bunk and surveyed the social order of the dorm. Everyone seemed to be divided by racial groups. The only two places I saw mixed groups were in the blind corner where the guys were smoking and a table where some Black, white and Hispanic men were studying the bible.

The first person to walk over to my bunk and spark up a conversation was an older man; he looked as if he might be in his seventies. He introduced himself as Marvin, explained that he was a Christian, and offered me a seat at the table where they were discussing the bible. He told me about a prayer circle at five o'clock every evening. I politely declined his offer and he faded away as easily as he had approached. Ten minutes later another guy—a white guy who seemed to be in his late fifties—came over and offered me a bible. I dismissed him handily, wondering to myself why these dudes were thinking I needed prayer or protection.

Later that night, they called recreation and we all went outside. I noticed a pod of Bloods out on the rec yard. Several of my original homeboys, as well as a couple of others I had initiated over the years, were there. They filled me in on the way things were and their beef with the Crips. Immediately I told them that I wasn't banging on lock; I was preoccupied with getting out of there, not getting into more trouble. I told them that I did not feel obligated to anybody I had not had a relationship with before prison. A couple of Bloods from Fifth Ward, a neighborhood in Houston, took exception to that. I explained to them that what happened to us in Frazier Courts was a hood-thing, a beef based on avenging my cousins and friends. I was not about to go around like some dim-witted tin soldier pledging allegiance to dudes I knew nothing about and tripping with others who had done nothing to me. The Fifth Ward Bloods made it clear that this left me to fend for myself. They walked off, leaving me with my real homies, guys I knew from way back. But I soon learned that they, too, were taking what I'd said the wrong way. I was baffled as to why anybody thought I would show up and take part in something as stupid as banging on lock. The seriousness of those conversations were my first glimpses into this new world called prison.

The next morning, I slept through the breakfast call—which oc-curred daily at 3:00 a.m.—and I would have missed the work call, too, had it not been for a guy called Phats. He hit my bunk at 5:00 a.m. and hollered "Ho Squad" in my ear—it was going to take time, I realized, to get used to working for a group with this ridiculous nickname. Phats told me they were calling my bunk and they'd write me up if I didn't turn out. I scrambled out of bed and headed out without any breakfast.

Phats was kind of like the character in Alex Haley's novel *Roots* who helps to talk Kunta Kinte—that would be me in this situation—through the process of slave acceptance. While an officer on a horse yelled at all of us to get a hoe and get in the ditch, happily overzealous inmates were chanting and singing songs to the beat of the cadence of our hoes cutting the grass. In my mind, I was leading a Nat Turner rebellion vision. Phats kept saying, "Slow down"—you had to stay in rhythm with everyone else cutting at the same time—and "There's only fifteen minutes left before a water break." It was dehumanizing work, void of any skill transferable to free society.

We worked until 10:30 a.m., when we were given a break to eat so that we could be ready to get back out in the fields by 12:00 p.m. I was hungry enough to eat a twelve-piece box of Kentucky Fried Chicken by myself—but when I saw the food that was being served, I was taken aback. They called it pork noodle casserole, but it looked more like dog vomit, accompanied by some old cornbread, beans, carrots, and greens. I shook my head but stuck my tray out anyway. The inmate serving the food gave me a pitiful half a scoop of the whole mess. I actually ate the concoction and then, starving as I was, wished I had more.

Phats sat next to me, eating only the beans and a peanut butter sandwich. I thought he must be a vegetarian, until I heard another inmate greet him with "Assalamu Alaikum," and I realized he was a Muslim, which meant the pork was off limits for him. The inmate asked Phats if he would be going to service later that day; Phats nodded, saying he'd be there. Immediately I asked if I could go too. I wasn't trying to join; I just didn't want to go back to the fields or sit in the hot dorms. Phats said he'd have to check with the Imam, the person who led the prayers, and then he asked if I was a Muslim. "No," I said, "but *Malcolm X* is my favorite movie of all time." Phats chuckled and said, "I was asking because you act like one. But you ain't got to be Muslim to get on the list, you just have to respect our services."

"Well, let me get on the list then!" I replied.

As we were walking out of the chow hall, Phats spotted Willie Fareed Fleming, the Imam he had mentioned, coming down the bowling alley. He was holding a pile of books and prayer rugs in his hands as he walked to the chapel. Phats called to him; they exchanged an Arabic greeting, "As salaam alaikum," and then Phats explained to him that I wanted to attend the prayer service that day.

Fareed looked at me and asked, "You're Kiddo, right?" I nodded, a little uneasy that he knew my name. He said, "You have a lot of homies who talk good about you." The phrase, *believe none of what you hear and only half of what you see* ran through my mind. "Yeah, we all know each other well in Frazier Courts," I replied. He was quiet for a moment and then said, "I'll see you at service."

And that is how I first ended up going to the Muslim service.

10

CROSSROADS

There was a brand-new chapel on the Hutchins Unit. It was clean and air conditioned, and the Muslims were allowed to use it on Fridays. An officer was present in the building, although the Muslims registered everyone as they came in and ran the services very professionally. It was impressive. Most impressive, though, was the pristine quiet. There had to be somewhere between sixty to eighty men in the chapel on the day I went to services—the same men who made such a clatter and ruckus at mealtime or during recreation—but you could have heard a pin drop as everybody filed in and joined the ranks sitting on the floor. I felt immediately calmer. Still, I assumed that most of the guys, like me, were there because they preferred to be chilling in the air conditioning rather than working in the fields.

It didn't take long before the silence prompted me to hear the voice inside that had been muted since I'd arrived. I began to think about Kenyada. I'd been hoping for it to be possible that somehow, with her staying in Pleasant Grove, away from my mother's house, she wouldn't run into Deborah. I had managed to keep the two women separate from—and unaware of—each other even until this point. I had been a coward. I was still being a coward. I had been planning to break things off with Deborah before Kenyada got pregnant—but then I hadn't been able to summon the energy to do so once I found myself preparing for Kenyada to have my baby *and* fighting to stay out of prison. Now that I actually was in prison, I hadn't yet let Deborah go because I was weak and needy, wanting all of the support I could get. But I was also beginning to realize that it was just this kind of childish thinking that had to come to an end if I was going to grow into the role of the father I hoped to be.

Fareed broke the silence in the room. He was a warm and positive person, but, with his small stature and chubby build, he didn't seem to me like someone who could deliver an impact with his lectures. His talk that day was about the story of Oedipus from Greek mythology. Oedipus left his adoptive parents when he was a young man to go out into the world in order to find his true identity. As the story goes, Fareed explained, Oedipus soon found himself at a crossroads—literally. He arrived at a point in the road where he could go north, east, south or west.

While standing there, contemplating his next move, a chariot charged toward him. Oedipus—feeling fearless or foolish, I can't say—refused to move. When the charioteer and one of the passengers stepped down to ask why he wouldn't move, a fight ensued, and Oedipus killed them both. An old man came out the back of the chariot and tried to strike Oedipus with his scepter. Oedipus skillfully brought his life to an end too. That last man, as Oedipus discovered later, was his real father: Laius, King of Thebes.

Not yet aware of this, however, Oedipus followed the road along which the chariot came. Along the way, Oedipus encountered a Sphinx that tauntingly and hauntingly offered him a riddle that no previous traveler had been able to answer—and they had all died as a result. The Sphinx asked, "What comes in on all fours, moves around on two, and then goes out on three?" Oedipus pondered for a while and then responded, "Man. He crawls on all fours as an infant; walks on two legs as an adult; and leans on a stick in old age." Furious that Oedipus had bested her, the Sphinx hurled herself off a cliff. All the people came out and celebrated the end of the Sphinx; they rewarded Oedipus by making him the new King of Thebes and offered him the widowed queen's hand in marriage. The people loved him, and Oedipus forgot his quest to know himself. In the end, we learned that a Prophet had foretold that Oedipus would kill his father and marry his mother. When Oedipus learned that prediction had come true—he had indeed killed his father and was now married to his own mother—he was sickened to insanity.

After Fareed had finished explaining the myth, he asked: "Are you, like Oedipus, at the crossroads of your life? Are you fearless or foolish? We know that you will fight and have great skill and a propensity for violence. We know that if you put your mind to any problem, you will find a solution. Oedipus made a great ruler, as will you, but his problem was that he didn't know who he was. Is it possible to know who you are without knowing God? Almighty Allah."

I'd had a cavalier attitude about everything in life: drugs, drive-bys, causing my mother pain again and again, cheating on the mother of my child—all of it. It felt like I'd been speeding down the freeway at a hundred miles per hour, unable to do anything but make split-second decisions until now. I was slowing down, exiting, and feeling the rush of it all fading away behind me, queasy with the idea that there had been no basis for it.

Fareed shifted his narrative slightly, saying, "Today, many of you are searching the scrolls of Black history, desperately trying to find an identity that you like. Well, you need to know that anyone who takes a journey but doesn't know where they are going may just feel at home in a nice spot, kind of like Oedipus. But I believe it is impossible to know yourself without first knowing God, Almighty Allah. To know yourself, you need to first know the God who created you and then you will find your purpose, reason, and direction, along with the manual that will help you operate at your maximum potential.

"To know God is to find God, and when you find him, you will find that He is Most Gracious, Most Merciful. He is Oft Forgiving. He accepts repentance. He loves us unconditionally. He is the Truth. And the Truth is the quickest way to God, the Truth of what you did and who you did it to; the Truth of what's wrong with you and what you know you need to do to be right; the Truth about right or wrong. Find the Truth and obey it and you will find God Almighty Allah and Submit to him."

When the men all around me got down on their knees and started to pray, I found that I, too, wanted to pray. I, too, wanted to be truthful, perhaps even seek God, but on that day, I stood back and watched.

The next morning was Saturday—no 3:00 a.m. wakeup call— but I was up early anyway, waiting to be called for a visit. When they did finally call my name, I tried to be measured and calm, but really, I felt like sprinting all the way to the visiting room. I'd only been in prison for forty-eight hours, but walking down that corridor, I felt as if I was being permitted to walk back through the years to a life I'd left long ago. I was about to kiss Kenyada and hold our baby girl. When I was processed in the visiting room, though, I learned that

I could not have a contact visit—meaning glass would be dividing me from Kenyada and we would speak by phone—since we weren't legally married. I would have to make it through a thirty-day waiting period before I could even touch Kenyada or hold our baby. When I walked to the glass window and saw Kenyada with our daughter, Tileyah, in her arms, it made me feel so confined, controlled—locked up. Kenyada's eyes spoke for her; her gaze was flat and dutiful, as if to say, "If I didn't love you, I would not be doing this." That, in juxtaposition with her beauty and poise, broke my heart.

We spent the first part of the visit talking about my fears, which came tumbling out of me: "Do you have enough money? Is the truck doing fine? Is anyone helping you with the baby? Has Tileyah been sick? Do you think you'll be able to get back in school in the fall?" After she answered all my questions, it was her turn. Apparently, she'd been hearing an earful about me since I'd been locked up. Was I the leader of a gang? Did I get all my stuff from selling dope? Did I go to concerts and church with a girl named Deborah? I offered an emphatic, "No, no, and hell no!" to every question. I couldn't gather myself. I had never seen Kenyada be so assertive. In many ways, this was my first time really seeing Kenyada at all. Out in the free world, there had been so many moving parts; there was always another thing to look after or hook up or shake down—it was easy for me to skim over the finer points of Kenyada's character. But now that she had a baby to look after, there was no time for my shenanigans. Kenyada wasn't putting up with any more of my excuses. I blamed the rumors on all the haters who were saying things behind my back that they would never say in front of my face. By the end of the visit, she wore a familiar look of anguish, like I'd seen so often on my mother's face. She promised to be back the next week, and I wanted her to come back—but I also felt disgusted with myself that I hadn't been able to tell the truth.

Not long after that, one late night in my cell, I picked up a pen and felt the urge to write my father. The idea had been stirring in me and I acted on it; if prison had given me anything at this point, it was time to consider my life and the ability to start putting one foot in front of the other based on my better instincts. I had a thought that if I could get back to the beginning, to the vanishing point of my childhood, and hear the story from my father's side, maybe I could set myself straight in adulthood. "I don't know if you will get this letter but if you do, write me back," was all I could think to put down. I signed it, "Your Son."

———————◆———————

Coming Out of the Cave

In prison, there is a popular saying: "commissary is necessary," and it is absolutely, one hundred percent true. The commissary is the prison store and carries sodas, packaged meats, soups, chips, correspondence materials, coffee—the list goes on. I had a couple thousand dollars on the books, so once I made commissary, I was able to buy some food—allowing me to skip the depressing chow hall—and some deodorant so that I could stand the smell of myself in my cell. The only hygienic items available to me before then had been five small bars of soap, some baking soda for toothpaste, and a sawed-off toothbrush.

If you're fortunate enough to have enough money on the books to go to commissary—and, honestly, few in prison are—you're also able to push your name up to the top of the wait list for Windham school district, which is the Texas Department of Criminal Justice school system. By this, I mean I was able to barter with an inmate who worked in the administrative building—I bought him coffee, ice cream, and ramen noodles—and he fixed it so my name magically appeared at the top of the wait list. Getting into school meant that I could get out of the fields into an air-conditioned classroom during the peak hours of the summer months. Needless to say, I was eager to make this happen. At the time of my incarceration, the administration encouraged inmates who had not finished high school upon arrival in prison—as I had not—to attend Windham when their names came up on the list. There were classes for every level of dropout, from the grade one to grade twelve. Seeing fifty- and sixty-year-old men taking classes for the illiterate was humbling. It was also clear to me that more than 80 percent of the inmates were high school dropouts, and only a small number of those men were actually trying to address the problem.

But once I started, I felt like I was getting back to my roots as a devoted student; I soaked up as much as I could. I enrolled in Computer Business Application, College Prep, and Parenting and still wanted more. The library became my refuge. The librarian, a white woman in her sixties, took note of my inquisitiveness and talked with me about the books I was reading every time I visited. She could hold her own on every subject, from the origins of slavery to the molecular origin of photosynthetic eukaryotes (which, as she taught me, is just a fancy way of saying algae and plants). We became good friends; she treated me like a human being and a seeker. She became my first white friend; I noticed she held no racist feelings toward me. It made me feel a pride and ambition I hadn't felt since was a kid when I'd show off the straight As on my report card to my grandmother and mother. The librarian offered me first right of refusal to all the new books donated to the prison so that I'd have a shot at them before they were put out on offer to the rest of the inmates.

The books that I read not only became a lifeline in prison but also a way in which, for the first time, I was able to put my experiences into some kind of context. Every narrative offered a new brushstroke to the portrait that was emerging in my mind—of history and my seemingly inevitable position in it.

The first book I read in prison was *The Autobiography of Malcolm X*, based on a series of interviews between Malcolm X and the journalist Alex Haley. I was blown away to find someone whose life allowed an entry into understanding my own up to this point, as well as offering an idea of how to exit such circumstances. After a rough childhood—his father was killed when Malcolm was six years old; his mother was committed to a mental hospital when he was twelve (and *still* he did well in school)—the man had been given ten years for larceny and breaking and entering at age twenty. He converted to Islam in prison. His story, of course, resonated. How could it not? But, more than anything, I was impressed that he had gone from being "Detroit Red," his nickname when he lived in Harlem—where he'd moved when he was eighteen years old, becoming a hustler, dope dealer, gambler, pimp, and numbers runner for mobsters—to speaking at Oxford University. Alex Haley recounted that Malcolm X read fourteen hours a day in prison. I knew I wanted to do the same thing— no, not just that, I wanted to compete! I wanted to beat Malcolm X! I began to read, on the days when I hadn't been assigned a job, sixteen hours a day. I sat at the little table in the day room reading all day and night, to the point that other inmates would sometimes grab all my books and say, "You're going to bust your brain, come to the yard!" Malcolm X gave me the first taste that transformation was real—it could happen even without a formal education—and that made me hungry for more.

Frederick Douglass, Booker T. Washington, W.E.B. Dubois—I read them all. I learned a great deal about Black history, finally, but I also gained a new perspective on my prison experience. Douglass was especially inspiring because, despite being born a slave and working in the fields from "can see to can't see"—being caught, in other words, in a prison sentence far greater than my own—he was still able to raise himself up.

I studied the early American street gangs in New York in the 1700s and 1800s, consisting mainly of English, Irish, and German immigrants. There was an Irish American street gang called the Dead Rabbits—apparently so named because someone threw a dead rabbit into the middle of the room during one of their meetings— roaming the lower East Side of New York prior to the Civil War; the Chinese had gangs, some of them also prominent in New York City, like the Flying Dragons and the Ghost Shadows—these two clashed over turf wars and also got heavily into heroin trafficking after the Italian American mafia lost the trade during the 1980s. Of course, the mafia is its own famous gang, which was highly influential in my own childhood. We all came up adoring the gangsta movies and thinking that the G-Code of Al "Scarface" Capone and John Gotti was mighty impressive. The common denominator among all these gangs then—and now—is that their members originally came from poverty-stricken communities, and they are all selling something illegal or practicing straight-up extortion.

I also tore through psychologist Na'im Akbar's books; he's known for bringing an Afrocentric approach to psychology and a focus on the intellectual oppression of African Americans. I came to these books through the Muslim community in prison—they were fascinated by Akbar's theories. The one that stood out the most to me was *Breaking the Chains of Psychological Slavery*, published in 1970, before I was born, although it felt so relevant to my life it was as if Akbar were sitting in the room, talking with me. He offers a profound, and un-settling, narrative about the ways in which the horrendous treatment of slaves still informs the mindset of many African Americans today. That is, the negative thinking and uncertainty that plagues many of us continues to hold us back from true liberation. Akbar also discusses how to break this chain of mental slavery. It actually made my heart hurt to ponder whether I'd had a slave mentality. Why had I so readily taken life as it came? There had been a few I knew who had managed to sidestep gang life, who had a firm enough sense of themselves from early on not to get caught up in the streets. I remembered my mother's explosive furies—and finally realized the terror she was fighting against. Other books also opened my eyes to the narrow vision I'd had for my life up to that point. Dennis Kimbro's *Think and Grow Rich: A Black Choice* is basically a leadership book, but his simple concepts, such as *what you think about grows*—and a negative mindset will perpetuate negative circumstances—made me reexamine my entire existence. Throughout, I had primarily thought about drug selling and repping the hood and living a dope boy's life-style—and these ideas had impoverished my mind because I'd never even considered *what success might look like* outside of that.

At the suggestion of the librarian, I read a book I might never have come across otherwise: *Man's Search for Meaning* by Viktor Frankl. It was about Frankl's three-year experience in Auschwitz and other Nazi concentration camps, where some of the cruelest torture I'd ever heard about occurred. Every day, Frankl struggled to survive—not just physically, but in his spirit, as he was plunged into an abyss of hopelessness. "The one thing you can't take away from me is the way I choose to respond to what you do to me," Frankl writes. "The last of one's freedom is to choose one's attitude in any given circumstances." It helped me navigate the harshness and uncertainties of prison. The Hutchins Unit, even at its most ugly, couldn't compare to anything that Frankl had gone through. That book also nudged me closer to the realization that faith and trust in God were paramount for finding a sense of peace during that time.

Finally, in Plato's *Republic*, I read the Allegory of the Cave, describing three prisoners chained to some rocks in a cave; their heads are tied so they cannot look at anything but the stone wall in front of them. Day in and day out, they stare at the shadows that play across this wall, projected from *things* passing in front of a fire behind them. These prisoners have been there since birth and so have never seen anything but what is immediately in front of them in the cave. These prisoners become proficient in naming the shadows. That is the only reality they know, so they do not want to leave. But, as Plato imagines, if one of the prisoners were set free to leave the cave, outside, "slowly, his eyes would adjust to the light of the sun," and he would also begin to understand that what he then sees are the real people and things, the very world that he'd known until then as mere shadows. Upon his return to the cave, "he would try and convince [the other prisoners] of this newfound reality," wishing that he could bring them out of the cave to experience the world as it existed beyond their limited scope. This prisoner acts as a philosopher, perceiving and understanding higher levels of reality, coming to know the truth; his fellow inmates represent those he has to help. I was discovering a new truth, a desire to expose others to that truth and ultimately free them from the shadows of the game we all had been taught.

One morning, I awoke to slamming doors, followed by a loudspeaker announcement, repeating over and over: "Lockdown, rack up, and catch your bunk." I was still groggy and didn't understand the severity of what was happening. I got down from my bunk to go urinate. The next thing I remember, a tall female officer was reprimanding me. "Stop pissing," she said in a razor-sharp tone, "and get back on your bunk. Count time."

After I was finished, I slowly walked back toward my cell. When I passed Phat's bunk, he told me that there had been a gang fight at the church and somebody had been badly hurt. That's all he knew—but he said this kind of shutdown could last for a day or thirty days. During that time, the administration does a shakedown of the whole unit, to be sure there are no hidden weapons, such as a makeshift knife or a toothbrush whittled to a sharp point, to lessen the threat of another gang fight. So I settled into my bunk with a book, realizing that we might be here for a while.

By night's end, the word came round that the Crips had jumped a seventeen-year-old Blood with only three years to serve. My heart started racing when I heard this. There was a young Blood, about seventeen or so, who'd been badgering me since I got to prison. I didn't know him, but he knew me by reputation. Whenever I'd walk by his dorm, on my way to chow or church, he'd run to the window and bang on it to get my attention. For some reason, he always asked to see my pictures. I guess he knew that friends of mine, Bloods from Frazier Courts, had been sending me photos. I never wanted to give any of them to him—not because I didn't want him to see them but because I had observed that he was the only Blood in a dorm full of Crips. I could sense something was brewing there; something just did not feel right. But this little guy—he was very small for his age, and he seemed naive too—was persistent as hell. So I finally did show him some pictures and then I moved on. Now I wondered if this was the same kid everyone was saying had been stomped and kicked—by

Crips wearing steel-toe boots—until he was unconscious. Later, I was able to confirm that it was indeed him and he had died. By week's end, I learned that he was a schoolmate and friend of my younger brother. It made me sick to think of this little guy—so committed to the Bloods he was begging me to see photos of homies he didn't even know—was now dead for no reason but that he'd pledged his allegiance to the gang. It also made me think about how my younger brother could be in the streets right now calling himself a Blood, living after my example. I knew that my mother wouldn't be able to take me being in prison *and* her younger son dying from a stray bullet. More and more I was seeing in slow motion this flawed thinking of being in the game.

The three Crips who'd killed the kid were immediately locked up and sent back to the county jail for new charges. A young brother was dead, and three other young brothers would never go home to see their families again. I knew what Blood leadership would be thinking—once we came off lockdown, my homies would be planning revenge. But I also knew how out of control our loyalty to this foolish, propped-up ideology had become. The more time I'd spent in prison, the quieter my mind had become—and with all the time I had to think, I hadn't been able to find a good a reason for why I was in there. I'd been blindly fumbling through life, tossed from one thing to the next, one drug deal to the next, one bullet away from death— sometimes I woke up in a cold sweat, amazed that I had somehow slipped through it with my life. I suddenly realized we had been programmed to kill each other. I tried to rationalize why I needed to stay in the game, but I couldn't find an honest answer. Where I thought there was love, there was no love. Where I thought there was brotherhood, there was none. I thought repping the hood was a reason, but we didn't even own the hood, we rented it. No matter how political it seemed, the fact that we would still kill our brothers was ridiculous.

The Friday prayer service was packed. There were a lot of new people there—I figured the death of our young Blood had sent people looking for answers, or at least for company, in their sorrow. There were many more officers this time too. As always, though, the Muslim faithful operated like a well-oiled machine. They moved and handled their business quietly and efficiently while keeping brothers—many of them obviously from different sets—peaceful.

Fareed took the podium and asked: "Bismillallah ar rahman ar Rahim. Why did Cain kill his brother Abel?" He went on to talk about these biblical brothers and what kind of emotions, what kind of mindset, would lead one to take the life of another, his own family. Fareed said he'd thought a lot about this over the last week and had come to the conclusion that there were two things in Cain's nature that had led to Abel's death: arrogance and ignorance. "Cain was arrogant, and God knew he was arrogant, which is why he wouldn't accept Cain's offering. And feeling conceit and grandiosity, Cain felt justified beating his brother to death. Why did those three young men kill the other young man here at the gate of the chapel? It wasn't because he had a red rag and they had a blue rag. No, it was because they were so arrogant; so full of conceit, of grandiose ideas about themselves, that they felt they had a right to beat him into nonexistence in order to heighten their own existence." Those words pierced me like a sword. "It is called self-destruction," he continued. "We, America's Black men, are the most likely to die from heart attack, stroke, diabetes, hypertension, smoking, and drug overdose. And now we are most likely to die at the hands of another Black man. The murder rate is so high among us that some people are calling us an endangered species because more of us are on lock or being killed or addicted to drugs than are in college. Our reason for this madness is colors? He's wearing red and you're decked out in blue. Somebody tell me, how did the devil brainwash you like that? You arrogantly and ignorantly represent this color because you are ignorant to who you are in truth. Cause in truth you are God's most prized creation. You are a peacemaker, the son of a mother who has high hopes in you being the one to elevate your family to another sphere of life. In truth you are a caring and compassionate analytical thinker whose mind can change our people's pain into prosperity. In truth you are a savior and a son of the Most High God." Again, this message resonated with my reflections and observations.

Fareed then made the invitation. "Join us in the morning as we begin a unity rap session after our classes. It's easy to talk peace, but for peace to become real, we need to come together and make it a reality."

Fareed had far exceeded my initial expectations—I'd not pegged him early on as the intellectual and charismatic orator he turned out to be—and my curiosity was piqued when he mentioned the rap session. The next morning, I went to check it out. The first two brothers who rapped represented two different types of emerging styles. They were off the chain—as raw and talented as some of the famous rappers I'd listened to over the years—yet their message was one of harmony and the lyrics were, of course, cleaned up. The next couple of homies did something completely different. They jammed a song called "My Brother Ain't a Color." I will never forget it. They had such a flow, and they were so alive, we couldn't help but all get up on our feet, fists pumping, jamming and singing along. "My brotha ain't a color, blood is from another motha. God made him my brotha.

Together we can go further than we can riding with this color."

I couldn't get the rap session out my head. The only thing I had ever heard before that had come close to it was one song that came out in 1988 called "Self-Destruction" by a group of stars like Kool Moe Dee, MC Lyte, Heavy D, Chuck D, Doug E. Fresh, and Flavor Flav from Public Enemy; they all came together for a Stop the Violence movement formed by the rapper KRS-One. Public Enemy had a positive message for that moment, but for the most part rap was segmented and adversarial, and it was full of insults and threats. It was amazing for me to see this music that had been so influential in my life turned toward the positive without losing its impact. I decided to send an invite to the brothers who had performed at the session and ask them to meet up at my dorm to rap. We had to do it on the lowdown because it wasn't allowed—but still, they all showed up. We took over the smoker's corner—the blind corner where we were hidden from view—and, with one guy laying down a beat on the table with two pencils, everyone began to vibe. In that moment, I saw brothers from different sets and neighborhoods and cities come together to escape the realities of prison. We were all in the moment, absorbing the rap. I immediately knew that I would be doing this again; this was not only a way to get through my prison time, but it showed me a path toward bringing people together instead of creating more divisiveness. I befriended everyone enjoying that moment regardless of gang or race.

Lately, I'd felt like whenever I'd ask a homie arriving fresh off the chain, "How much time you got?" too many responded with twenty, forty, sixty, even ninety-nine years. We all shared the same common denominators—we were dropouts, gangbangers, dealers—but, somehow, I'd only gotten seven years. I was one of the founders of the first Blood gang back in the day and had been proud as hell of that—but now I was starting to feel indirectly responsible for every one of those kids who would be lucky to taste freedom again by the time they were old men. "OG Kiddo, I was out there putting in work for the hood," they'd say, "making them Crips respect this gang 415." I could see the die-hard loyalty in their eyes. When I told them I wasn't banging anymore, trying to impart the difficult revelations that had been crashing over me, the disillusioned look on their faces always rested hard on my spirit.

A month or so into my time in prison, I was walking down the bowling alley when Fareed caught up to me from behind. "Assalamu Alaikum, li'l brother," he said in greeting.

"What's up?" I replied.

"Li'l brother, I been paying attention and listening to the talk around the compound," he said, getting right to the point as usual. "There are a lot of people who look up to you around here." Even though my experiences with the Muslim prayer services had already sunk deep into me by then, I was reluctant to get caught up with whatever Fareed was about to propose.

"Li'l brother, if you have the influence to lead all these brothers to do wrong," Fareed went on, "then within you also is the ability to lead them to do right. Li'l brother, you are a natural leader."

I had never heard anyone offer that kind of revelation about me before.

"I hear ya," I said nonchalantly, though I was humbled and a little taken aback that he'd been paying such close attention.

12

IN THE BELLY OF THE BEAST

On my twenty-first birthday, September 18, 1997, less than four months after I'd entered prison, I embraced Islam. I was attracted to the discipline and the search for knowledge it encouraged; those qualities had not only been lacking from my life before, they had also since made me feel more alive to my own possibilities, and the possibilities of the world, than I had ever felt in my life. I recited the Declaration of Faith, "La ilaha illAllah." Fareed administered it after the Friday prayer, as the entire Islamic community smiled and embraced me. As was his practice, Fareed concluded the oath by saying, "Live an Upright Life, Establish Peace wherever you go, Always Put Allah first and always reach back to pull another brother out of the clutches of evil as you have been freed from its grip."

Fareed and Phats had joined together to pick my Muslim name from attributes they saw in my character: "Anees Musa Shakur." Phats chose "Anees," which means *friend*; Fareed chose Musa Shakur, which translates as *deliverer of my people*, as well as *appreciative* and *thankful*.

"Chowtime!" an inmate screamed early one morning, walking up and down the hallway, beating on the dorm windows. I jumped off my bunk and headed for the dining area. I passed the officers, in their customary gray and blue uniforms and dark shades, standing by all the entrances and exits. During chow, inmates had a maximum of three minutes to eat their food and then leave. While I was hurrying along in the line to get my food, I heard someone yell my name. "Kiddo, what's up, OG?" I looked up and found D. Hall, a friend of mine from Edna Rowe. He was working in the kitchen. "What's up, Blood?" he asked, full of pride. I immediately told him I wasn't banging no more. "Nah, babe, you the OG," he said defiantly. "What you mean?"

I just shook my head and said, "I ain't with it no more, long story."

"Man, you one of the ones to start it, this 415 Blood gang," he pressed. "You can't quit."

I asked the brother to please respect my wishes. I knew I had to practice this new outlook.

The following day, I saw D. Hall during chow again—and, again, he pressured me on why I wasn't banging anymore. This time I was a bit more forceful in demanding he respect my choice. The other inmates were starting to pay attention to the commotion we were causing, so I backed off and got out of there quickly. Back in the dorms, I thought about why this situation was nagging at me so much. I felt conflicted as to how to handle the situation—there was a tug of war going on in me about how to stay loyal to my homies while also staying the course with myself—but one thing I knew was that if I truly meant what I was saying about giving up the gang, my boy D. Hall was going to be my test. That night I prayed, asking for acceptance—from others *and* from myself—that I no longer wanted to participate in that form of genocide.

The next morning, D. Hall gave me the Blood greeting as I waited in line for food at the chow hall. I took a deep breath and tried to restore the calm I'd achieved the night before. "Please respect what I told you," I said, as measured as I possibly could be. Immediately, D. Hall pounced on my remark: "Man, you the OG. I ain't 'bout to not call you anything else." Without thinking, I jumped over the counter onto his side of the kitchen and hit my friend dead in the eye. He fell to the ground with the most confused look on his face. The punch had cracked so loudly, so unexpectedly, everyone stopped. I stood frozen, staring down at my friend on the ground.

"I told you I ain't no damn gang member no more," I finally said.

This denouncement of the Blood lifestyle placed me in the position of being a neutron. This meant that the Bloods were not supposed to talk to me about gang business; it also meant that Crips had free range for harming me, since they knew they could do so without consequences. That was fine with me. I welcomed not having to contemplate whether or not I had to take someone out. I didn't want any part of it anymore. Meanwhile, my true homies never stopped kicking it with me. And I think just being known as one of the founders of the Bloods in Dallas paralyzed the others from trying to hurt me. They knew that if I had the balls to start a Blood gang in an all-Crip era, I was not to be tested. The implication of the incident inadvertently sent the message throughout the prison that I was serious about the denunciation.

It was a Thursday night when I was called for mail; I was sure it was from Kenyada. I jumped off my bunk with all the nonchalance that a brother who hadn't gotten a letter in a week could muster. When I looked at the name on the bulky envelope, my stomach flipped. I was glad, I wanted to smile, but I didn't know how exactly to receive a letter from my father. Inside, I found a twenty-six-page letter. I climbed back atop my bunk and started to read.

My father dove right in, telling me he loved me and never thought that he would have been away from me my whole life. He told me about what it was like for him in the late 1970's and how hard it was to get a job and how he pushed back against being considered a second-class citizen at the height of Jim Crow. I knew and understood. I was glad to find I wasn't holding anything against him as I read. Then he told me how proud he was of all the things he'd heard about me. My reputation had made it all the way to him in prison, specifically the Coffield Unit, a few years ago. Every time someone would ask him if he was Kiddo's dad, he said he smiled with pride, knowing that I was the leader of our hood and keeping it real. I felt uneasy about this misunderstanding. It gave me the bewildering sense of having outgrown my own mythic father, of seeing that he was unwittingly caught in the same trap I was now trying to scramble out of. Nowhere in the letter did my father ask the questions I'd anticipated in our first encounter. There was no "How is your mama?" or "Do you have any kids?" The man hadn't seen or talked to me for most of my life. Was he not curious? It was not my idea of how the first interaction with my father would go. Still, I spent the whole night writing him back and forgiving him of his absence.

Friday's Jummah prayer service had become an anticipated event. I began to look forward to Fareed's talks and the messages they conveyed, the unity among the men and the cherished moments of silence and seriousness. I can still remember just about every message that Fareed delivered back then because it honestly felt as if he knew my every thought. God was using him to speak to me. I hadn't yet realized that just about every other young brother in that room was going through the exact same thing as me.

"Never will Allah change the condition of a people until they change what is in their hearts." Fareed began that service with a verse from the Quran. "We suffer from poverty, illiteracy, gang infestation, and drugs mainly because we come from fatherless homes. The African American family in the hoods that we come from has been decimated. It's in shambles and survives as a shell of the structure that Almighty God Allah intended it to be. The fathers are nonexistent, the mothers are working away from the home twelve to fourteen hours a day, and the children are the victims of images and ideas of violence, sexual promiscuity, and drug use.

"Twenty years pass, and many times we don't realize that we are imitating our fathers. We have women who love us in a very selfish, nonproductive way, just like our fathers did. We have children we have abandoned, just as our fathers abandoned us . . . And many of us put the game and gangs before our children, women, and mothers. Just like our fathers. This resonated with the situation I was currently in. I was juggling three women, in prison not being present for my newborn daughter. I chose the game over education. I was in essence repeating my own father's footsteps.

"Never will our condition change until we change what is in our heart, and if you haven't realized it yet, your actions are witness to what's in your heart."

It was as if Fareed had sliced into my mind, seen my thoughts, and was responding personally to them. Still, a voice inside of me scolded, *I was a product of the violence; I sold drugs. I was more loyal to my homies and the gang than I had even been to my own mother; worst of all, I abandoned my family, just as my own father had done to us.*

When I left the service, I was consumed with telling Kenyada at our visit the next morning that I had been wrong for playing with her feelings and her future. By the time I made it to my dorm, I was rehearsing the painful confession I would make to Kenyada. I would tell her the truth, apologize, and promise never to do it again. I had to make this right.

When I arrived in the visitation area, though, I found it was Deborah and my mother, holding Tileyah on her lap. I tried to smile, to keep up an enthusiastic front. I sat down and picked up the phone and pressed my hand against the glass in front of me. My mother put her hand to mine in a gesture of affection, but her expression was stern.

Tileyah was dressed in pink. While I listened as my mother told me things that didn't interest me, my daughter's eyes never left my face. Occasionally, she began to laugh uncontrollably; those innocent outbursts pierced me as I began to realize there was likely no chance that the three of us would build a family together. Finally, I asked softly, "Is Kenyada okay?"

My mother looked down at Tileyah and began to rock her as she said, "Kenyada said she wouldn't be coming to visit you again, but she wasn't going to deny you the love of your daughter."

"When did she say this?" I asked. "What happened?"

"I am not going to get involved in the mess you have going on," my mother said firmly. "But I will say that it's the same thing your father did. I never found out about all his mess and other women until he was locked up."

I looked at Tileyah in her arms and wanted to say something, but all I could do was try to breathe and fake a smile. For once, I was glad for the thick glass separating us; it gave me some cover. I spoke briefly with Deborah and ended the visit.

Back at the dorm, I worked out until I didn't have anything left in me. I saw Kenyada's face everywhere. I heard her asking me *Why?* I asked myself *Why?* I took a shower and got in my bunk under the sheets and cried until I fell asleep. I was utterly alone, and I had done it to myself.

13

THE DISEASE

In prison, watching the news was a daily ritual for me. It was my primary source for what was happening on the streets—and a measure by which I viewed the growing distance between my old life and the mindset I was developing in prison. Every day there was another report about a gang shooting, either in Dallas or somewhere else in the country. Drive-bys were wounding innocent children and the elderly. The Feds were increasingly locking up gang members and giving them federal time. Not everyone shared this viewing habit with me, however, so I had to fight to extract snippets from the real world. The day room was usually a chaotic buzz of activity and noise, and it was nearly impossible to hear the television over the chaos—until, that is, the soap operas came on. Then you better not make a sound. Suddenly, these burly dudes—ready to jump on anyone at the slightest offense—would cross their legs and sip their coffee and chatter about the latest on *One Life to Live* or *General Hospital*. When the news was on, though, it was right back to the bedlam, and I would have to strain to hear. The day room became like a college classroom for me; I would routinely hold sessions with different races and gangs discussing commonalities, squashing beefs, repairing our families. On a micro level I got a glimpse of unity and brotherhood with each session.

One day, though, I happened to catch the news on a blessedly quiet afternoon in the day room, and a local story came on about gang interventions—and suddenly I was seeing my cousins Super Dave and Rainbow on TV! They were flanking a guy named Omar, who was being interviewed about his initiative toward ending gang violence. The three of them were standing in Frazier Courts. I couldn't believe my eyes. After the shock of seeing my family on the news, I began to settle in and listen to what this guy, Omar, had to say. It looked as if his eyes were closed. He was on point, talking about the senseless violence and bringing former gang members over to the side of peacemakers in order to reform and revitalize East Dallas. I felt like he was speaking my mind. I could only imagine Rainbow and Super Dave were involved with this too—and it gave me a sense of the universe doing its work to think that we had all started down this new path together without even realizing it. I was fortunate enough to have money on my books, which allowed me to spread it and then have the heart to not throw the leftovers away, which was customary in prison, but instead to feed those I saw were hungry, which opened up conversations and friendships with inmates who could be considered my enemies. I befriended members of the Crips, the Aryan nation, and the Mexican mafia. We were all learning to trust each other. I was doing gang intervention without fully realizing it.

The next day I went to my first AA/NA meeting. Because I'd been charged with possession with intent to deliver, this was mandatory, but I'd also voluntarily signed up as one of the many classes I picked when I first got into Windham. I'd been told the parole board looked at this choice favorably when it came time for them to make a decision. The turnout at the meeting was huge. We were gathered in a classroom; the seats had been arranged to create an enormous circle. I recognized several ex-clients from my dealing days.

The volunteer hosting the class was a diminutive, leathery-faced woman. She definitely looked like she had been through a few wars. She had a raspy voice and was short on words. "We've come to admit that our lives are unmanageable when we use drugs and alcohol," she said by way of an icebreaker. Then everybody started reciting the rules and a prayer. "God grant me the Serenity to accept the things I cannot change, the Courage to change the things I can, and the Wisdom to know the difference." Soon after, a guy I knew from Frazier Courts stood up and began to share. "Hi, I am Jason. I am an addict." The room responded in unison, "Hi, Jason."

I actually not only knew him—I also knew his daughters, cousins, and ex-wife. The man had been a crack smoker since I started selling it back when I was thirteen. When he introduced himself as Jason, an addict, I wanted him to look at me so I could smile, indicating that I knew him. But he wouldn't look my way. As he began to tell his story, I realized why.

"This is my fourth time here on the Hutchins Unit for possession in two years. Some of you know me, some of you don't," he said. "I'm an addict who has tried to work the program, and this last time I thought I had it down. I had a great sponsor and I had gotten a job at Parkland Hospital in the transportation department. I had regained the trust of my wife and moved back in with her and my two daughters. Everything was going well. I was making it to free-world meetings and even going to church with my mother. After five months on the job, I finally had some extra money. My wife had gone to the country for a family reunion, and I was home alone with about six hundred dollars.

"The evening started with some Miller beer and a weed-smoking classmate. It ended with an eightball of cocaine and some females who wanted to party. The next day I was so mad at myself but said I would go to work and then to a meeting and get myself back on track. I never made it to the meeting that evening. Instead, I spent the rest of the money I had on an encore performance with the same females.

"When my wife came back the following day, she sensed something was wrong but gave me the benefit of the doubt. The next night, I left our home with her diamond and gold necklace to head to the crack house to get an eightball." He turned his eyes and looked at me. I realized *I* had taken that necklace for the eightball and given it to Kenyada. The man continued. "That began the homelessness and spiraling out of control. In December 1996, I stole the TV out of my daughter's room. It is the single worst thing I have ever done in my life. When I was arrested on New Year's Eve, I was cold, dirty, and down to 143 pounds. The crack had won again. When my wife found out where I was, she served me with divorce papers. And with that being my fourth possession case, the DA wanted me to do prison time, so I got seven years."

As he finished his talk, I was the one who didn't want to make eye contact. Everyone else was murmuring, "Thank you for sharing." I didn't know what to do or say, but, at the same time, I felt if I had been him, I would've kept that to myself.

The volunteer was gracious and kind, telling him that everybody doesn't get it right the first, second, third, fourth, or even tenth time, but they keep on trying until they do. Another man got up to speak—an elderly Black man from Paris, Texas, who was so exceptionally thin I had to believe he was ill, perhaps with AIDS at the tail end of the epidemic. I could hardly stand the sight of his ravaged body, so I put my head down while he spoke. He said that he had been homeless for two years and addicted to crack. He had no money, so, he said, "all the big dope dealers would let me do they cars because I was good, and they would give me ten dollars and a bump." I knew he was telling the truth because we did the same in Dallas. The police stopped him one night and asked him to rat out one of the dealers and tell them whether he had a gun in his car, but the old man wouldn't do it. Soon after, the cops stopped and busted him for carrying a crack pipe. "But I didn't think nothing of it," he went on, "because I didn't have no crack. When I went to court, though, they said they were offering me twenty-five years because of my past record. I thought, *Twenty-five years for a crack pipe is too much*. But they wouldn't come off the number. Then I went to trial, and they gave me sixty years and one day." That got me to lift my head up. Sixty years for a crack pipe? I was a twenty-one-year-old ex-dealer hearing the horrors, pain, and shame of addicted people for the first time—and I was not prepared for the anguish of their real lives.

The next person to speak was a middle-aged Hispanic man who looked as if he'd never done a day of drugs in his life. He was clean cut, thick and robust, as if he had just rolled out of the gym. Once he began to talk, I noticed he was very articulate. This was his eighth DWI, and, this time, his recklessness had sent a senior citizen to the hospital. He'd gotten twelve years for vehicular assault. He said he thought about suicide every day because he couldn't live in this world with the disease he had. As he went on, I realized that he wasn't referring to a physical disease but was actually talking about alcoholism. It had never occurred to me to think of alcoholism as a disease. You could buy liquor at the store; how could it be a drug or cause such serious repercussions? Not only did I not drink, myself, I'd only ever smoked weed a couple of times. I didn't like the effect that it had on me; I did *not* like being out of control. It was hard enough for me to understand why people allowed crack to annihilate their lives; it was unthinkable that some beer or wine might ruin someone. So when this guy said that drinking was the disease that had destroyed his life, I couldn't help myself. I spontaneously let out a burst of laughter.

Immediately, the volunteer stormed over to me, looking as fierce as Mike Tyson; she put her finger in my face and yelled, "Get out, get *out!*" As I rose to my feet, I saw the disdain on everyone's faces. But they'd heard the story just like I'd heard it: the guy was blaming his drinking on a disease!

Once we were outside in the hallway, the volunteer let me have it. She said, "You are no better than anyone in that room. The only difference is that they have the courage to share their secrets and you keep yours perfumed and covered under that smirk and smile that looks as fake as jewelry."

I literally felt about two feet tall. This woman—transformed from a tiny woman who looked as if she had been through the ringer herself to a superior force able to put me down in one blow—knocked the ignorance right out of me. I'd been given, I realized, an incisive glimpse into the lives that had been going on all around me as I'd been dealing—lives I had played a part in helping to demolish. AA had provided another subtle, pivotal lesson in prison; I was sorry that I hadn't been able to open to it until it was too late. I was not allowed to return to another AA meeting.

Being in prison starting at twenty-one years of age was a loss for me. I knew it was a loss. As I read book after book, I could not justify my incarceration. Prison was not a rite of passage for me. It was emphatically a loss. But every time I recited the Sura from the Quran it reminded me of a new reality that was coming into view.

Every leader I had read about had this in common: faith. "Mankind's history has proved from one era to another," as Malcolm X states in his autobiography, "that the true criterion of leadership is spiritual." Martin Luther King once stated, "Show me how to take who I am, who I want to be, and what I can do and use it for a purpose greater than myself." Practicing Islam, praying five times a day, had led me to listen more carefully to my fears, thoughts, hopes, and desires. Reciting the Quran had opened a new level of self-examination, helping me to realign my thinking, morals, and aspirations with the ways of the righteous.

My favorite chapter from the Quran to recite was Sura 103:

By the Token of Time Through the Ages
Verily man is loss. Except those who have Faith,
Do Righteous Deeds and join together in The Mutual
Teaching of Truth, Patience and Constancy.

I was slowly shedding more than a decade of the indoctrination I'd received as a survivalist growing up in the hood; I'd been programmed to be less than honest when it was convenient and to place money above all else. Searching for Truth, however, introduced me to altruism and galvanized my ability to empathize with all people— not just those in my immediate world. I was motivated to accept truth no matter where I found it.

Throughout, the exemplar of righteousness for me was Fareed. I knew he wasn't perfect, but he practiced to the best of his ability.

We began to hang out daily on the rec yard. I had no idea until then how much he handled daily as the Islamic leader. Every day as we arrived on the yard, a series of problems were presented to him to be solved. One brother was being taken advantage of, another was at the point of suicide; a new brother in the community claiming innocence needed pro bono legal work done; two gangs were on the brink of war. And there were always racial issues to be addressed.

Fareed brought solutions, solutions, solutions. It was the only way his mind processed things. Even when his detractors were trying to assassinate his character, he tried to find a way to help them when he could have easily returned the hate. I observed his every move. He offered a stark contrast to gang leadership, where the answer was always violence; hate was met with hate; if I didn't know you, I wouldn't help you, and if it didn't make money, it didn't make sense.

Fareed very rarely talked about himself. What I did not know was that he was close to forty and had come out of a very bad adoptive family situation when he was a child. He once told me that all his life God had sent strong men to mentor him when he was lost, and now he was just paying it forward in hopes that I would one day do the same.

14

THE CIRCLE OF KINGS

Fareed led a leadership class called the "Circle of Kings." The premise was that each member was considered a king. And, as kings do, they were asked to find solutions for the problems in our culture. In the group, each member was asked to champion an issue—to research it, articulate the complexities, and then offer solutions to be questioned by the group. Fareed explained that this was his version of the Socratic method: he and the inmates engaged in these argumentative dialogues designed to cultivate critical thinking. Fareed asked me to join and clarified that it would mean that we wouldn't hang out informally during the week as we'd been doing. But he felt I was ready for the challenge. He said it would require discipline and work on my part, but I also felt his confidence in me, and that urged me forward.

I chose gangs as my issue; Fareed had been researching AIDS; some of the other members had taken on poverty, broken families, drug addiction, political disempowerment, and reducing the dropout rate.

Joining the leadership class was also my first brush with gang intervention work, although at that time I didn't realize it. As background research, I began to ask some of the other inmates the questions I was looking into for my presentation. I would gather a group together and ask things like "Why is gang banging a poor people's problem?" or "Why do we resort to selling drugs as opposed to going to school?" Each answer was followed by *why*.

These questions always led to intense, heartfelt discussions about how we comprised a generation of gang bangers and drug dealers— but now that we were in our twenties, no longer fearful teenagers living a lie in the hope of being accepted, we could denounce that and try to be true to our own selves. You'd be surprised how quickly even the toughest gang member will let his guard down, and articulate compassionate truths, when the circumstances allow for it.

I found that my time in the Circle of Kings helped me to not only draw out my ideas but to really press against them. I'd grown so much intellectually and spiritually in such a short time, but I was also new to the process of learning. I was so enthusiastic; I hadn't yet realized that every thought or theory that came to me was essentially a newborn; each one needed thought and care and guidance before it was ready to go out in the world.

A couple of months in, Fareed scheduled me to give my first Friday lecture and lead the prayer. I was nervous but I was also motivated; I had so much I wanted to share. If anything, when the day came, I was *over* prepared; I'd memorized and rehearsed every word of my lecture over and over. The topic was *forgiveness*. The idea of myself at the podium delivering this lecture was very important to me. I wanted everyone to see me in that new light. I wanted to be a vessel of God delivering truth to my brothers in the struggle.

Everyone filed in in order, as with any other service. I surveyed the chapel, trying to get the feel and rhythm of the flow that day. Everyone took off their shoes, as is customary for Muslim services, became quiet, and settled cross-legged on the floor. I walked to the podium, all the brothers staring dead at me. The guards in the back of the chapel were eyeing me as well, attentive to what I was about to say. I glanced down at my notes. I had prepared a lecture about the idiosyncrasies of prison and forgiving oneself, addressing the experience at large; I felt that I could speak to the disappointments and revelations and trapped longings of a generation of men. But as I stood looking out at the audience and then back to my speech, I suddenly realized that I'd come to this as a doctor might put together a medical speech. I had diagnosed the problem and now I was delivering the cure. I had been separating myself from the problem as I'd thought about what I had to say, but suddenly I knew that the patient was *me*. I was as much a part of the men staring back at me as they were of me. Looking into the audience, I felt as if I were shouldering all their pain and weight, even the ones who had not yet allowed themselves to feel it, even the ones that would never find a way to break through to this.

I could not find it in me to speak a single word. In fact, I can only remember one thing from that moment: a profound desire to say, "I'm sorry." Instead, I began to weep. In that moment I unlocked the door to my own vulnerability. Something highly forbidden in prison. And I believe the brothers seated before me didn't break the seriousness of the moment by laughing or making fun because, for an instant, together, we understood the magnitude of our situation.

Fareed walked to the podium, hugged me, gently guided me to sit down alongside the others, and then delivered a lecture and led the prayer. He ended by telling everyone that next week I would have a message for them that they would never forget. The following week, more than one hundred and fifty brothers showed up. That time, I asked God to speak through me, to help me get to the core of why we were so divided as people and to enlighten my brothers about how to have true love for humanity through forgiveness—and the message of unity and redemption easily flowed from my mouth.

The red blood flowing through your veins makes you my brother. Your mind and the ability to forgive faults, wrongs, and misunderstandings make you my brother. And the Spirit of God that dwells in you and inspires you to love the stranger and an ex-enemy is what makes you my brother. Always. Darkness cannot exist where light shows up. My brothers, you are the light!

I led the prayer and felt redeemed. To my surprise, more than twenty brothers came forward to join Islam and denounce gangs that day.

At Fareed's request, I began to teach on the Hutchins Unit every Saturday morning. I created a standard lecture called Education Equals Economic Escape. One morning, the Islamic chaplain Iman Shabazz dropped by while I was speaking. He was impressed and stayed after the service to talk with me and other leaders of our Circle of Kings. He asked if I would be interested in teaching at a unit with a very serious gang problem. He said he'd seen something in us that he felt would really help save some brothers who badly needed a new way of thinking. I asked him if it would help me make parole. "Brother Anees, I can't promise you that," he said, "but I can say that Allah would be pleased with you. Allah is the best of payers." I asked for a few days to think about it.

Later that night, lying on my bunk, I asked myself two questions: 1) Was I ready to leave this laid-back unit close to my house that allowed for more visits from my family and Tileyah? 2) Was God preparing me for something I didn't quite understand at the moment? I knew I was decent at delivering the message, but I wasn't sure I was ready to leave my comforts for a disciplinary unit with gang killings almost every day. And yet, three days later, I was agreeing to do it and, three weeks after that, I was on my way to the George Beto One Unit in Palestine, which housed three thousand of the most violent inmates in Texas.

On the bus ride to the unit, riding down the long, narrow road lined with trees that stood taller than I'd ever seen and seemingly endless fields, toward a prison deep in the woods, my fears began to grow. Everyone on the bus was stone silent as we journeyed toward the "gladiator's playground," as the place was once described by a reporter, "a hardcore joint—even as prisons go." The gang wars were intense; stabbings, murders and rape were common; the usual ritual upon introduction was to fight. Perhaps the best way to envision the difference between the Hutchins Unit and Beto One is to think of Hutchins as a house kitten and Beto One as a lion.

I was most concerned that after word hit that I was on the unit— and that I was no longer banging—I would have to deal with either Bloods trying to prove something or Crips trying to get their stripes. I was not about to play any games or tolerate any disrespect because of my choice to denounce the gang, to be an upright man for my daughter and family rather than participate in genocide.

In Texas, whenever you arrive at a new unit you must take part in an interview with the classification officer; this is called the classification process. I recalled the interview I'd done at the Hutchins Unit and didn't anticipate that I would enjoy this one much either. But when the officer met me, he shook my hand enthusiastically and said that he considered me "a model offender." He commended me for having performed excellently on Hutchins with my school and work. He looked at the other men in the room and then said, "I am recommending Lucky be sent to the Trustee camp."

To my surprise, the Trustee camp was outside the gates of the regular unit. It was basically a work camp, and it was as quiet as a funeral home. No gates or barbed wire fences surrounded it. Feeling God's grace and mercy guiding me, I immediately made my prayers and prepared to go and meet the Muslim community on the unit.

Once I arrived in the building part of the prison, though, it was immediately obvious why the chaplain at Hutchins had thought my teachings would be a good fit. Beto was in the grips of a gang explosion. Not just among Crips and Bloods but among all the active prison gangs present.

Teaching on Beto, as I began to do every Sunday morning, called for more patience and tact; I had to be strategic about how I delivered the hard truths. I made a pledge to always speak truth to power and the poor. It was a must for the brothers to retain or regain dignity and respect. My focus was sharp, and my character was intact. And word spread fast throughout the Unit of my teachings. Brothers would tell me that my style was relatable and made sense to them. They didn't see me as a religious fanatic trying to proselytize everyone I encountered, they explained, as some other brothers had done in the past. They complained that they had been too pious to identify with them and their struggle to truly make a change. I think it may have helped that I never forgot where I came from. If God had patience with me, despite all the wrong things I had done, who was I not to have patience with others? I wrote letters, counseled, befriended everyone, and encouraged anyone regardless of race or gang affiliation.

Leaving the infirmary one morning, a young brother approached me and offered me an Arabic greeting often used by Muslims.

"Wa'alaykumu s-salem," he said. "Are you brother Anees that everyone is talking about?"

"That would be me," I replied. "But what is everyone saying?"

"Nothing bad, bruh," he said, laughing, "just that you are bringing a fresh message that's got the brothers on the wings really thinking about life choices, so it's all good." I smiled and asked how I could help him.

He told me that he had taken his Shahada—the Muslim declaration of faith—years ago. But, he continued, he had since been excommunicated from the Muslim brotherhood. At one point in his life, he explained, he had taken part in homosexual activities, and leadership had gotten wind of it; they banned him from attending any services or affiliation with Islam. But the young brother wanted badly to come back into the fold. He was genuinely seeking my help. I could sense the sincerity of his request. He needed help, he said, and he thought if anyone could help redeem him, I was the one. My next words to him were, "First ask God for forgiveness, then forgive yourself. Turn away from that sin and spend the rest of your life living for Allah." Before we parted ways, I told him to come to Jummah prayer on Friday, where we could meet with the leadership council together.

After service on Friday, the leadership council always met in a dorm room outside the chapel. As the young brother and I entered the room, I instantly sensed the animosity toward him. Eighty percent of the fifteen brothers present were serving life sentences. I told the council that our young brother had something to say. It was rather awkward for me to do this, as I was still fairly new to the unit and brotherhood. But I also knew my leadership style had to be assertive in this environment. The young man began by apologizing for his unMuslim-like conduct and asked for mercy and a chance to get back on his *din*, an Arabic term for the way of life adopted by Muslims to comply with divine law.

Before the young brother could even finish what he was saying, however, an elder Muslim brother became enraged and yelled, "Brother, don't you know the Quran says, homosexuality is punishable by death. Didn't we ban you? Why are you here? You are not a Muslim anymore."

I instinctively knew that the elder's view wasn't right. I hadn't seen that particular law enacted, and I felt furious to see this man abuse his leadership in that way. Why was he torturing this young man who begged to get his life back on track, who so obviously wanted, *needed*, to be allowed back into the community?

"If the Quran says homosexuality is punishable by death and you are a believer, then kill him! Kill him!" I shouted, staring him in his eyes. The entire leadership council looked on in total confusion. "If the Quran says death, then kill him," I said again, and as I did I stepped in front of the young brother, staring the elder in his eyes. I didn't know if he felt that he would have to kill me to get to the young brother, but my point was made.

The elder stood silent, looking bewildered. The room was quiet. Finally, he stepped back. "Only God has the power to redeem and grant mercy," I said. "Our God asks that we repent and turn away from our sins. He is Oft Forgiving and Most Merciful." This was a powerful moment for me. It was the first time I'd found myself having to defend someone *against* the religion, and it would later play a distinct role in my understanding of myself as more of a broad spiritualist. I didn't want to be judge, jury, and executioner when it came to someone else's character. Everyone is entitled to redemption regardless of their transgressions. I internalized that. I came to believe that spirituality has a universal moral code, as opposed to being constrained or dictated by the dogma of religion. If we are all one, I decided, then, we are all one.

One brother from the leadership council stepped forward and greeted our young brother with the traditional Arabic saying "As-salamu alaykum," meaning, "Peace be upon you." But he also meant *welcome back*. And then the rest of the council followed, one after the other. I walked out of the chapel and headed to the Trustee camp through the back gate. It seemed like a long walk that day. I humbly prayed that none of the leadership council would go back on their word and hurt the young brother. I looked up into the sky and smiled. I breathed in the fresh air and enjoyed the leaves blowing in the wind. Somehow, I felt the universe was thanking me for being an upright citizen that day. I got so caught up in the moment that I forgot I was in prison and didn't notice the perimeter car creeping up on me; a loud horn blasted as the occupant yelled, "Get back on the sidewalk, inmate!" And I quickly snapped back into reality.

Walking to the visitor's room, I felt nervous about my first visit with Kesha. I hadn't seen her in close to five years, since we were teens really, and I had no idea if she would look different—or if I would seem visibly changed to her. We'd reconnected through letters—she'd written me when she ran into Clay, who'd told her I'd landed in prison. She wrote to me, curious about how my life had unfolded since we'd spent that short time together way back when—and we'd come close to falling in love. As I entered, I looked around at all the families and couples' chatting, kids running back and forth to the vending machines, and I saw a beautiful Black woman—the adult version of the girl I'd once known, with more of a shadow behind her eyes—sitting by herself. I walked up to the glass and grabbed the phone. With an engaging smile, she said casually, "Well, hello." We talked for the next two hours about our lives, our plans for the future, and what was happening outside the gates in Dallas. After that, I relied on Kesha's letters to keep my spirit alive during the daily grind of prison life. Every letter, laced with a little of her perfume, allowed me to be free for a moment or two.

One day, as I was leaving the chapel, I passed a group of brothers and one of them called out, "K-Ray?" I laughed and explained to a guy who looked familiar to me that K-Ray was my cousin. "I'm Kiddo," I told him. The guy's face lit up—but, still, I couldn't place him. "I'm Vito from Sunchase," he said, reminding me of his nickname and referring to some apartments in Pleasant Grove. I flashed back to him as a kid. His real name was Gary Walker; we'd been friends in elementary and junior high. As we started to catch up, the guards told us to keep moving, so I suggested that he meet me at Taleem service the following weekend.

After my lecture the following Sunday, Vito approached me again. This time, he was taken aback in a different way. "When everyone was talking about the ex-Blood leader from East Dallas who is now a Muslim bringing the heat in services," he said, "I would have never guessed in a thousand years it was you!" I responded, "Yes, well, it's a long story and road. But God is good."

Vito began coming to Muslim service regularly after that. We would catch up and talk about the past and, in so doing, we developed a friendship once again. One day, out of nowhere, he hit me with something completely unexpected: He told me that he was innocent of the crime he was serving time for in prison. He had fifty-five years for a murder he said he knew nothing about other than it had occurred in Sunchase Apartments.

I immediately thought about Fareed and the guys who used to come to him on the yard claiming to be innocent. I recalled how he would listen and listen and listen, carefully taking in their stories. Eventually, either they would contradict themselves or prove to be innocent. I decided I would extend the same patience and impartiality to Vito, hoping never to come across inconsistencies in his story. In the meantime, I encouraged Vito to go to the law library and research if there were any legal means to return him home—or at least get him back in court. Every week after that, I would ask Vito to again tell me the story of how he was convicted of a murder that he hadn't committed; each week he told me the same story without deviation. The woman who died had owed Vito twenty dollars—her sister had loaned her the money to pay Vito back. On her way to him to pay the money, however, she was murdered. When Vito heard about her death, he went to her house the next day to find out what had happened, and he encountered the slain woman's sister. She began interrogating him, edging toward accusing him, and then the police detectives rushed to make an arrest based on her claims. The more Vito described what had happened, the more I became convinced of his innocence. However, I also knew that, without new information about his case leading to the real killer or who the real killer was, Vito had little more he could do to get out of Beto. I worried for him. It was hard enough to maintain your sanity if you were *guilty* of the crime that had landed you there. I told Vito that God would reveal some information about his case.

Then, a few months after I'd first run into Vito, a chain bus of new inmates arrived at the unit. A guy who also used to hang in Sunchase Apartments was in the new crew. One day, out of nowhere, in the midst of a random conversation with Vito, he mentioned he had two friends who'd killed a dope fiend lady in Sunchase. Without knowing anything about Vito's case, amazingly, he'd provided Vito with details that would have been impossible to know about this particular murder unless he'd actually learned about it from someone on the inside. He described how the lady had been shot and where the two killers had run to hide out afterward—and he actually gave Vito the names of the guys he said had done it. It gave Vito new hope—but he needed someone on the outside to track the men down. I promised to help him. Somehow, I knew in my heart that one day I would. My parting words were, "I will not leave you here. If I can't be real with myself then I can't be real with you."

Not long after, on my third time up before the parole board, having been rejected twice before, I was told that I had finally been approved. I would be going home in nine months. As the time closed in on me going home, I began to say my goodbyes to the brothers I'd taught at Beto. None of us quite understand the full impact of our experience together. I'd come in leery of their violent natures, but I was leaving with a soaring sense of their promise—so much so, it hurt my heart to imagine how many of them would never return home. Some of them had not yet truly forgiven themselves for their crimes, and I gave them my last encouragements to do so; I also reminded the inmates of their responsibility to the younger ones coming in. To my utter surprise, many of them cried when we talked about my days there coming to an end. The brothers said with me leaving, the prison wouldn't be the same. As crazy as it may sound, and as much as I had been hell-bent on getting back to my life, I was heartbroken to leave them behind. And of course, the naysayers were saying that because I was now a felon it would be hard to be accepted back into society. I assured them that the X on my back would be what qualified me to do the work.

And then, one day—a day I truly couldn't imagine until it actually happened—I was on the chain coming home.

15

GETTING OUT OF THE CAN

On April 14, 2000, I was one of 476 men released from the Walls Unit in Huntsville. I was given some clothes from South Africa, shoes from Thailand, and a hundred dollar check—with the promise of another hundred if I reported to my parole officer within seventy-two hours. Walking out the doors of prison, down the steps and onto the streets into a free society offered a particular feeling of exhilaration that I think only other once-caged people can ever understand. Some of my fellow inmates were smiling joyously while others were dead serious, focused only on getting to the bus station and as far away as possible from the prison town. I was experiencing my own particular sense of anxious freedom—I felt the thrill, of course, of walking back into the world a free man, but this was also partnered with a sense of responsibility. I had to stand firm with the changes I'd made in myself.

"Kiddo! Kiddo!"

Kesha was just ahead of me, in front of her black 1999 Mercedes, waving and calling my name.

I had an urge to run over to her and give her a deep, passionate kiss. At the same time, I was also fighting to keep the tears in my eyes from falling. I was still uncomfortable with public displays of raw emotion; I managed to walk over to her with a little swag. I hugged and kissed her while beating back my tears, trying to maintain some self-control.

I was one of the blessed ones—to walk out of prison into a black Mercedes with tan leather seats and 2-Pac's greatest hits playing. Kesha and I began to roll down the highway holding hands. I was so thankful. Most people don't understand—I was yet to grasp this myself—the environmental and social acclimation that a person has to make after prison. People sometimes expect that friends and family getting out of prison are the same people or will be ready to party—but I found I had a strong and unexpected desire to be quiet.

As Kesha and I rolled and made small talk, every time there was a break in the conversation, my emotions began to well up. I couldn't explain it, even to myself. I was finally free, but the thought of those last conversations with the brothers I was leaving behind in prison were etched in my mind. I needed to hear my thoughts. I went in one way and came out another way. Something definitely happened in there. I wasn't the same person.

My plan with Kesha was to get something to eat from Two Podners Soul Food Restaurant—which was, at that time, around the corner from Frazier Courts. Ironically, as soon as we exited Lamar Street and started to drive through the hood, 2Pac's song "Change" started playing. *I got love for my brother but we can never go nowhere/ Unless we share with each other/We gotta start makin' changes/Learn to see me as a brother instead of two distant strangers/And that's how it's supposed to be/How can the Devil take a brother if he's close to me?* The first familiar person I saw was an ex-customer of mine; he was pushing a grocery cart down the sidewalk. Though he was a bit thinner and frailer, to me he felt like a reminder of how the hood remains so stubbornly the same. We pushed down Colonial Street; memories of all the times I'd hung out at the pool hall there surfaced. The streets were filled with addicts, people hanging out, drinking and smoking, others playing cards under a shade tree. I told Kesha to make a right on Malcolm X and we drove past the notorious Little World food store. That place had been the backdrop to more robberies, murders, and arrests than anyone cared to remember. It hadn't changed much either: people were jumping in and out of their cars, running in and out the store to make their deals. I reflected back on years ago, when I came out of that store and was shot at by a Crip who was no more than eight feet away. Lucky for me, the guy was a terrible shot, so he didn't hit me—or anyone else—before wildly driving off.

As we rolled down Hatcher Street, I thought of how much I had been through in this neighborhood. There were more abandoned buildings and dilapidated houses on every street. I had a thought that 2Pac's "Change" was possibly a reminder from God of my commitment to try to change this neighborhood I'd played a hand in decimating in the first place.

Here you go, let's see what you do.

By the time we pulled into the restaurant, tears were streaming down my face. Kesha asked me if I was okay. I took off my shades, pulled some tissues out of the console, and said, "I guess I didn't realize how bad things were." For the first time in my life, I saw East Dallas plainly for what it had always been: an impoverished, gang-infested, drug-selling neighborhood.

As we walked into Two Podners, people started to recognize me. A couple of homies greeted me with something along the lines of,

"Dang, you gained weight!" The smell of oxtails, fried chicken, and banana pudding overwhelmed me as Kesha and I stood in line to be served. As I was preparing to order just about everything on the menu, Kesha's phone rang. She smiled and handed me the phone. It was Clay. He welcomed me back home and told me that whatever I needed to get comfortable, he had me. He also mentioned that everyone was headed to the Kappa beach party—which gathers about 35,000 people every year in Galveston, Texas, to cruise the sea wall, to drink, eat, and listen to music—and I could ride with him if I wanted. Kesha heard every word of our conversation. She was practically stalking the conversation. I let Clay know that I wouldn't be doing any partying or hanging out. I realized that paroling to Kesha's place in Desoto—a nearby suburb that was far enough from all the people and things that could get me into trouble—would be a good thing.

The next morning, I was up before 5:00 a.m., kneeling and praying by the east window of the bedroom. The silence of the house helped me to bring back the scriptures that I had memorized in prison. So many of the books that I'd read—that had put me on a path—were echoing loudly in my mind. The voices of Fareed and Vito were clear, too, but my own voice was the most astonishing to me. *I will not return to gang banging or crime*, I found myself inwardly promising. *I will help change this community that I've had a hand in destroying.* As the rising sun beamed rays of light through the window, my heart began to flood as I realized that I would finally be able to hold and kiss my daughter Tileyah for the first time.

16

GOD'S PLAN

Three years after I was convicted and forty days after my release from prison, I was searching for a job, contemplating going to college and thinking about what I would major in if I did. Making those plans felt hopeful but also daunting. I had no idea how to enact such good intentions. In prison, I'd understood God's plan to be all encompassing. I'd been so relieved to be held by a power larger than myself, to imagine that I was not alone in steering my unwieldy fate, I'd allowed myself a somewhat simple view of what a spiritual life was and what it could do for me. And it had worked while I was in jail: I'd developed a moral code that I could abide by, and the changes had felt radical and immediate. But now that I was out, what exactly God's plan *was* had become a more perplexing question. I was struggling to understand what this phrase that had given me such solace in prison actually meant when applied to practical life circumstances. I knew that I wanted to reach out a hand to my homies—particularly the ones that were still dealing and hustling as I'd once done—and lead my community. I knew that I wanted to keep learning, stay straight, and earn my keep legitimately. I had been so focused on transformation within me and building my faith inside. But I didn't know quite what faith should, or would, look like now that I was trying to execute a plan in the real world.

Just seeing the hood again in person had made a huge impression on me. Driving daily into South Dallas from the suburb of Desoto helped me realize how lucky I was to be free and healthy. I also noticed how the manicured lawns, uniformity of shapes, and cleanliness did something good to my mind. But it also made me worry all the more about my friends and cousins and everyone else still caught up in the same cycle of drugs and violence, one bullet away from going to prison or dying.

Summer was approaching. The escalation in violence in Dallas was playing out across the culture at large, with an increase in gang fighting and crimes occurring across the country. Meanwhile, the rivalry between Frazier Courts and Park Row had been menacingly renamed as a Crips and Bloods beef—and it was filling the streets of Dallas with blood. But even if the names were different, the rules of engagement were still the same: If you were from one neighborhood—be it Blood or Crip territory—and caught in the other, you would be beaten, maimed, or killed.

Late one evening, as I was pulling into my mother's house in East Dallas, my cousins Rainbow and Super Dave, also original 415 founders, were waiting for me outside. They, indeed, had been—and still were—working for the brother I'd seen on the news named Omar. Omar, they'd told me, had a contract hiring ex-OGs in Dallas to revitalize the community in East Dallas. He wanted to put them to work as mentors to young kids getting into the same dangerous situations they'd once been in; he also wanted to make former OGs part of the solution before they might contribute to the problem again. They'd explained that Omar had an idea for how to go about doing this; it was similar to the kind of thing I'd been talking about wanting to do. And they'd mentioned me to Omar, too, explaining that I'd been a leader on both sides—I'd once led the Bloods into violence and crime and now I wanted to lead them out. They told me Omar had himself been nurtured by a community leader and had gone on to be hired by the Texas Youth Commission—where I'd nearly gone myself after I was sentenced to juvie—as its first ever gang intervention specialist. After working there for five years, he'd been inspired by Bob Woodson—a civil rights activist who'd founded the Woodson Center, an organization that trains and funds community-based leaders—to take his antigang message to the streets and put his plan into action. It was so similar to what I'd been thinking about as a way forward. I couldn't believe someone else had already forged this path ahead of me. I knew I had to meet this guy, so I'd asked my cousins to set up a meeting. Rainbow and Super Dave told me that Omar wanted to talk and that he was available to meet as soon as I wanted.

When Omar and I got together later that evening in Frazier Courts, we shook hands as he said, "Everybody's telling me I need to meet you to put together a peace treaty." At twenty-seven years old, he was only three years older than me, but he came across almost as if he didn't belong to any age at all. He had a dignified authority about him. "I want to bring the OGs of each set together to stop the violence," he told me, "and help the youngsters see that what was started years ago was wrong. It was wrong then and it's wrong now." Listening to him, I felt a momentary sense of déjà vu, as if we'd had this conversation before, until I realized that he was actually just articulating the thoughts that had been roaming my mind for so long in prison.

When Omar and I met a second time, he explained that he'd seen peace achieved among gangs in prisons across America—mainly in California, where the Crips and Bloods had started. We also talked about the origin stories of the Crips; I say *stories* because there are many. Omar explained that Crips was an acronym for Community Revolution in Progress—and that way back when, in 1969, they'd formed in order to protect the community. Some say that the Crips were an offshoot of the Black Panthers; others say that the name came from *cripple*, because the gang's early style included "pimp canes," with attention-grabbing handles, usually tipped in gold. Stanley Tookie Williams, who, along with Raymond Washington, was the cofounder of the gang, wrote in his memoir *Blue Rage, Black Redemption* that they'd actually first called themselves the Cribs, but they'd mispronounced it as Crips one night when they were drunk— and it stuck. In any case, Williams and Washington first brought together this soon-to-be-notorious gang as a form of self-protection for a group of teenagers whose L.A. neighborhood was under siege by other gangbangers. (Washington was killed in a shootout in 1979; Williams was executed in 2005 for the murders of four people he swore, until the day he died, he did not commit. Williams also began a crusade in prison to end gang violence; he was, as he put it, a "Paul Revere, warning youths about what is coming down the crooked paths.") How a group formed by two teenage boys as *refuge* ultimately became an unprecedented army of gun-wielding drug dealers spreading rage and grief and blood through the streets not only of California but the world was beyond Omar; his point, though, was that they weren't originally meant to be that way. They were first meant to offer guardianship and community to counter crime and violence. Which put an interesting spin on the peace we were trying to achieve—that it was the early intent of the Crips. Incidentally, the Bloods rose up for the same reason in 1972, except they were meant to provide protection from the Crips. So it was a self-perpetuating cycle of attack and defense. Omar and I both felt strongly that if we could find a way to break it—or at least break *in*, with the message that there was nothing left to this rivalry but unnecessary bloodshed— we'd be able to make real change.

Omar then talked to me about Vision Regeneration, an organization he was trying to get off the ground. I opened my folder and pulled out a program I'd written up while in prison, IMPACT. We both outlined a similar strategy of enlisting former gang members to help shut down the rampant crime and violence in certain areas of Dallas. We both agreed we shouldn't reinvent the wheel, and we vowed to bring Vision Regeneration to life. I was the product and Omar was the salesperson. He was Batman and I was Robin. Together we made a perfect package. He leaned back and smiled. It was in that moment we both knew our meeting was divine. Omar was from a different kind of background than me—he was a second-generation activist and spiritual leader; his father, who'd grown up in East Dallas, was a gangster turned preacher. But as we talked that night, we discovered that our fathers had actually known each other. In fact, Omar's father had been the preacher who'd presided over my uncle Lonnie's funeral, and he'd done the same at my grandmother and grandfather's funerals too. We smiled about this chance past connection and the thought of how strong our partnership could be and started to brainstorm about how to achieve peace in South Dallas. The main thrust of our plan was to bring together OGs from each set—the Crips and the Bloods—and announce to the community that the old rules of shoot, jump, and beat up on sight were over;

it was time to make peace. To make this happen we had to first get each set to agree. Then we had to get the OGs to meet and get the word out to past and present gang members that change was in effect.

I committed to getting the OGs of the 415 Bloods together. I suggested that we also do guerilla marketing by plastering the city buses that rolled through the neighborhood with our pictures advertising our message. Nobody would expect to see my face—especially alongside a call for peace—rolling through the hood. I thought that would make the call to arms to former, and current, gang members all the more effective. Omar thought it was a great idea, but he needed to get the right people to put the resources together to make it happen. Next, he would need to find an OG from the Crips who would help us out from their side. The conversation went like this: "Antong, let's go over to Park Row and find a Crip OG." I was like, "Say what? I didn't plan that far out. I only planned for my neighborhood, and, besides, that's suicide for me." Ten minutes later he convinced me. Our meeting was fruitful, and we left with a solid plan for getting started.

First, I needed to get the OGs of my old set to be ready to meet within ten days to set up an agreement for the peace treaty. The original 415 founders were all my childhood homies or cousins so I felt confident I could get them to commit. We'd always been real with one another. And we all knew that what the new generation was doing was *not* what we had originally started; people from all over the city were coming to join the Bloods now just for recognition or credentials.

During that week, as I was touching base with everybody for the upcoming meeting, I received a call from Omar saying that he'd gotten Dallas Area Rapid Transportation (DART) to donate spaces on their buses for our advertisements. He'd also secured the funding we needed to do the marketing campaign; he'd even gotten money for us to put up a couple of billboards. I was impressed by how quickly Omar had been able to get the city behind us and secure funding.

And on my end, as promised, a week and a half after my first meeting with Omar, I brought ten of the original members of 415 to a Boston Market restaurant near my house in Desoto to meet. Omar stood before our crowd and started by talking about the most recent shooting in our neighborhood, as well as other shootings that had taken place over the past three years. He talked about the parents in Frazier Courts and elsewhere who were afraid for their children to walk the streets. He talked about the fights and drive-bys after school and on school property and then he ended by citing the outlandish number of arrests that had occurred in South Dallas recently. His point was that no matter which side of the hood you were on, you were losing—*we* were losing. The community was losing its youth. Mothers were losing their babies. Youngsters were losing their lives and freedom, and the city was losing because, believe it or not, they were tired of locking everyone up to no avail.

The crowd was unusually quiet. Nobody could contest the truth of what Omar had just said. I was so impressed with the way that Omar had strode into a room full of rowdy gang members, all of them completely unaccustomed to the idea of a peace treaty, and commanded their attention. I was just waiting for the first homie to say, "I'm down," so I could chime in alongside them. I looked down respectfully, waiting through the silence; I wanted to give everyone the space they needed to process what was going through their heads.

"I don't mind giving my allegiance to the hood for a paycheck that equals forty-thousand," one of the OGs spoke up finally.

Then another one said, "If I get in the peace business, do I get at least sixty thousand?" Still another said he wouldn't do it for less than eighty-five thousand a year! Somehow my boys had gotten it into their heads that Omar had connections to some money people at City Hall—and they were *negotiating* what it would take for them to help us make peace. I was speechless.

As they continued foolishly bartering with Omar, I glanced out the window and caught sight of Omar's Honda Prelude surrounded by our cars; I had come in a red Corvette, the other guys had driven up in Lexuses, Cadillacs, BMWs, and Suburbans. I shook my head.

"Man, this ain't right. I ain't getting a dime out of this and I ain't asking for a dime either. I started this with y'all. *We* started this," I said. "But if it ain't in your heart to seek peace, then maybe you ain't the solution. I am down, and I'll help move the peace process forward."

Three of my homies agreed to stay and talk; the rest left. "I'm out of here," one friend said, breaking the silence after I spoke—paving the way for the others. "Nah, man, sorry," another had followed, shaking his head on his way out the door. They couldn't imagine doing something for free. I was so embarrassed, and I felt stupid too. What had I been thinking?

When the meeting was over and only Omar and I were left in the room, I tried to think of what I could say to him; I felt ashamed that I hadn't been able to get a stronger showing from friends I'd known my whole life. "That was really good!" Omar exclaimed, putting a hand on my shoulder and smiling wide. I looked at him: *Were we in the same meeting?* "Just to have them come at all and to be able to talk to them about what we are thinking and what we want to do," he said, reading my expression. "And three guys *stayed*. That is a victory, my friend."

A week and a half later, in the middle of June, I found myself in Omar's Honda Prelude headed to the Crips' stronghold in Park Row. I don't know what possessed me to get in the car and make the trip with Omar—other than we had no contacts with any OG Crips and Omar was not equipped with the street cred and history to make this trip alone. The closer we got to our destination, though, the more I started seriously rethinking doing that. I was behind enemy lines. I remembered being stomped almost to death by the Crips in front of Madison High School. I remembered being shot by them; in fact, the hit was more than likely *still* out on my head. Yet on that hot and humid day, I was getting out of a Honda Prelude, unarmed and un- announced, heading into the G.W. Works apartment complex on Al Lipscomb Way (formerly Grand Avenue), the stronghold of the 187 Crips in Park Row. We parked in front and walked around back. There was only one way in and one way out of the trap house the guys were in. This was by design: once you walked around back, they want to be outside ready for you when you came out—if it came to that.

I started sweating. Omar had been so confident when he'd con- vinced me to do this; it had felt like a nonnegotiable test of my lead- ership. But now here he was, in a suit and tie, looking like he was on a college campus walking to the lecture hall to give a talk. I wondered if I hadn't been clear enough with him about how quickly the situation could turn deadly.

Suddenly, a window opened, and somebody shouted, "It's Kiddo!"

Within seconds, all we heard were guns clocking. I was set to run, but Omar yelled, "Kiddo, put your hands up!"

The door popped open, and eight or nine men filed out with their hands on a Glock, burner, shotgun, .357, .45, or .38 automatic. Omar and I stood with our hands up, frozen. All I could think about in that moment was my prayers. This was, I realized, the high-wire act of faith: I had no idea what would happen next.

"Kiddo, what are you doing over here?" Grover, the OG speaking for them, said roughly, a single gold tooth gleaming as he did.

Omar spoke before I had a chance to open my mouth. "He came with me to ask you to ask your set to consider a peace treaty because the violence is out of control," he said, smooth as silk. I was amazed. My knees were about to buckle. I was more scared that they'd shoot me before I could answer why I was there, and I was about to pass out on top of it from the hundred-degree heat—but there was Omar with an opener at the ready.

"I just got home about a month ago and I'm not bangin' anymore." My mouth was unexpectedly dry as I spoke. "As a matter of fact, after seeing all of our homies on lock and the way the game is out of control, it has made me regret any and everything I ever did to start and set this off the way that it is. I apologize to you and your set for the past, but right now my focus is slowing this violence down to a halt so that our mamas and grandmamas can stop crying over all of their babies dying because of the game that ain't paying. We banging to a beat that has us all paying decades behind bars for the life we live on the streets."

Grover lowered his gun, and, slowly, the rest of his set followed suit.

Omar walked toward Grover and handed him his card. Grover, still with a mean mug look, turned it over in his hand. "I'll see what's up," he told Omar, "and I'll call you." At that moment I wanted to tell him I had Crip brothers in prison, but I didn't.

As we walked slowly on the path back to the car, I thanked God.

There was literally no other explanation for me being alive at that moment. Omar later said he strongly felt that if we immediately showed that we were not there to battle, there would be an opening for conversation. Actually, his exact words were, "You'd have to be a psychopath to shoot someone standing there with hands up, asking forgiveness." But I still attribute our survival in that situation to spiritual resolve, our willingness to face a perilous challenge, and our faith that if we approached it honestly, we would draw forth the essential compassion in us all. The courage it took for me to go into a neighborhood where I had previously done drive-bys—and the risk that I might meet someone still salty who wanted to take my life—showed a level of commitment that surprised even me. And the moment that Grover lowered his gun became the testament to how much what I was doing really mattered.

17

———◆———

FORGING FORGIVENESS

The month of July began with the DART buses rolling through my old neighborhood, advertising the peace summit. The faces of myself, my cousin Super Dave, and Ike-Moe, another former Blood member, were on the side of every bus traveling through South Dallas; a billboard with the same image hung on the side of the freeway.

This guerrilla-marketing strategy had, as we'd hoped, the whole community talking. But not all of it was good: the first reaction I heard was that people were saying we had somehow conned the transit authorities into giving us a big paycheck to stop the violence plaguing the bus routes of South Dallas. This rumor about what I was up to was the first of many to follow—until people finally realized that I was truly out there, pounding the pavement, sweating it out every day in my old neighborhood in East Dallas, advocating for peace. I went from apartment to apartment, house to house, park to park, meeting all the new 415 members who had emerged while I was incarcerated.

My message to them was that brutalizing and murdering had been going on since before we had even formed 415 in Frazier Courts, but we didn't have to keep it going. It was time for us to take control of our lives and stop the meaningless violence. Meanwhile, Grover was promoting the peace treaty in the Crip territory of the South Dallas Park Row neighborhood. It had taken surprisingly little persuasion to pull Grover over to our side after that first confrontation—when Omar had announced the peace treaty and I'd made my impromptu speech. Unbeknownst to us, he'd been turning over the same thoughts in his mind about the fighting and deaths getting out of hand. He remained skeptical of me for a little while, but he trusted Omar—and, after our initial meeting, he told him that he was tired of hustling and seeing the homies die.

Not long after that, Omar approached me about "my image." I was driving a brand-new red Corvette and still splurging on expensive jewelry and dressing flamboyantly. Simply put, Omar said I looked like I was still in the game. I hadn't thought about it that way, but I quickly realized that he was right. I was having a hard time convincing others of my internal transformation; it seemed reasonable to ask that I stop dressing the part as a first line of defense. Although Omar and I were still in the early stages of our friendship, I respected his coming to me with the truth rather than just listening to everybody gossip about it. I adjusted immediately. Omar and I literally began talking every single day and our friendship grew. Shortly after, Kesha and I called it quits.

Omar purchased and gave me a 1985 white Chevrolet station wagon that looked like it had been used to haul around hippies in the seventies. I sold my jewelry toward much-needed living expenses and started dressing down. The only thing I couldn't bring myself to change was my Jordans. But to be fair, I wore a hole in the bottom of them walking the streets of East Dallas.

Meanwhile Omar was pitching to donor friends who were supporting us behind the scenes. Some of the things he was getting done were hard to believe. He roped in some incredible collaborators: One donor spent an unprecedented amount of money to rent out Two Podners and buy barbecue for all of us—Crips and Bloods—to eat while we tried to hash out a plan to come together. J. McDonald Williams, chairman emeritus of Trammell Crow Company, a commercial real estate development and investment company and the founder of the Foundation for Community Empowerment (FCE), a nonprofit dedicated to transforming low-income neighborhoods in South Dallas, secured the historic Hall of State in Fair Park, where the State Fair of Texas is held every year, for us to host the peace summit we'd planned for the community after we'd successfully—or so we hoped—brought everyone together at Two Podners. Before Omar told me, it had never occurred to me that wealthy people from affluent neighborhoods were praying and hoping for our success, or aware of us at all.

By the end of July, I had walked my entire neighborhood at least ten times. I had been reacquainted with old schoolmates, girlfriends, and the families of so many of our homies on lock. I talked to the younger brothers and sisters of friends who'd been killed during the gang wars who were now left only with the reputations of their loved ones to remember them by. I talked with mamas, grandmas, and the baby mamas. I talked to business owners, sex workers, drug addicts, hustlers, dope boys, and homeowners trying to move out of the neighborhood.

After all the talking, meeting, and, most importantly, listening, the one thing that was common with everybody was that they wanted the crime and violence to stop. And, other than a few youngsters from Madison High School who'd had conflicts over the last year with some Crips, no one had anything to say about anybody from Park Row. It felt as if the time had come.

In the period leading up to the treaty, during the last week of July, Omar, Grover, Super Dave, and I discussed the need to be aware that we were fully responsible for this peace process. There would be no police or intervention from anyone else. *We* were the peacemakers. The realization of all that we'd been discussing for these last months now rested on our shoulders—and it was up to us to show that it could take place harmoniously.

A couple of days before the peace treaty, the teens began filing into Two Podners by 1:00 p.m. A couple of hours later, there were one hundred young people from each set: the Crips and Bloods, Park Row and Frazier Courts. Most of the groups were made up of young men, but a few were mixed, and there some were young couples too. The occasional parent or older person came through, surveying the scene, but mostly the crowd was made up of the teens we'd targeted. The point of starting early in the day was to allow everyone to just chill in the same area, eating and socializing, without any drama for the first couple of hours—and, so far, it was working. We intuitively knew love would arise out of this interaction and commonalities would beam while people were eating, just as it had in prison, and then spread.

As the blazing sun and blue skies gave way to dusk, Grover and I were in the parking lot of Two Podners, greeting the later arrivals, while Omar was inside working the room. The parking lot was now filled mostly with the older, serious shot callers of both sets. Omar, Grover, Super Dave, and I had breathed a collective sigh of relief when they had finally strolled in. Their presence was a must if this peace process to move forward. At the same time, though, they brought a new sense of barbed tension to the proceedings. Whereas the youngsters had been easily won over with good food and company, their elders were warier, surveying the members of the opposite gang suspiciously while also side-eyeing us. They couldn't quite tell if what we were up to was legitimate; nothing like this had ever happened before, and I'm sure many of them were wondering if they were being set up.

As Omar began to introduce the OGs from different sets inside, the sounds of a fight began to echo through the crowd outside. My heart dropped. As I raced through a group of people to see who was scuffling, I felt certain that I would find members of the Bloods and the Crips going at each other. A thousand scenarios, none of them good, went through my mind as I tried to calculate whether I could stop it before it got out of hand. *We're in way over our heads*, I thought as I pushed into the inner circle of the fight. But, to my utter confusion, I found Super Dave scuffling with a youngster from outside of the hood.

Apparently, li'l homie was upset about being jumped by a few of the Park Row gang members earlier in the year. When he began to taunt some of the Park Row set, Super Dave had forcefully told him that this meeting was about peace and letting the past be just that—the past. He called Super Dave a few choice names, and, soon enough, the two of them got into it. It had ended almost as quickly as it began, and I was left mostly grateful that it hadn't been a Blood fighting a Crip—but it was a difficult reminder that old habits really do die hard. Even though I still found it a daily struggle to stay the course, I was amazed that Dave hadn't been able to hold back at the peace treaty. There'd clearly been no real reason for the fight—it was just a young'un with a petty beef—and it put our leadership in a precarious place. I didn't want to pour gas on the fire, though, so I just patted Dave on the back and quickly ushered the kid away from him.

Meanwhile, a newscaster, a white woman possibly in her late forties, had arrived in a van that read ABC WORLD NEWS, along with her cameraman. I assumed Omar had invited her; I had no idea the press would be at this gathering. As members of both sets continued to roll into the parking lot, members were discreetly tucking their guns under their shirts, not wanting to enter the meeting unprotected. Meanwhile, the reporter was casually wandering around, chatting with the guys, asking if she could get photos of some of them together. While Grover and I stood at the front asking people to please put their guns back in their cars and come inside to eat, to listen and support the peace, I kept an eye on the reporter, who continued to act as if she'd just shown up at a school picnic. I wondered if she had any idea of the powder-keg situation we were all navigating.

I heard Omar inside telling stories and calming everyone down. Occasionally, I heard the entire restaurant break out in laughter. The ABC World News reporter strolled inside the restaurant, where she and her cameraman set up their cameras. Immediately, a couple of hustlers and D-Boys came to us to say they wouldn't participate if cameras were rolling, and we understood their hesitation. Grover and I told Omar; he spoke with the reporter, and she agreed to shut her cameras off for the time being. Outside, Suburbans, Cadillacs, and big-body Benzes were still creeping in, demanding attention. The bass out the window was carrying the tune to "Big Pimpin" by Jay-Z and UGK. When, finally, Grover, Dave, and I followed the last of the parking lot crowd into the restaurant and positioned ourselves by the door, Omar knew it was time to start.

The place was packed. The counters were filled; there was no room left against the wall, and some people were sitting doubled up in seats. Omar started by talking about a police report detailing the murder of a resident of Frazier Courts who was killed in 1972. "Do any of you know why this murder happened?" Omar asked the crowd. It had nothing to do with blue or red, Crips or Bloods, he said. He then listed a number of murders from the late seventies through the eighties and asked if any of us had anything to do with them or knew why they'd taken place. He looked at Grover and me directly, saying, "Y'all's era of Bloods started in the early nineties. Can either one of you tell us why it started?" We both shook our heads. I knew it wasn't important to answer that question; mainly it was rhetorical in Omar's line of reasoning.

"If you are going to die and lay your life down," Omar said, "shouldn't you know why? Why are our brothers and sisters killing each other? We live just blocks apart from each other. We literally share the same zip code. For some of us, the blood of our relatives flows through our veins. Yet there is a law between us that says if you get caught over on these streets you shall die."

The room was quiet. The ABC World News reporter was preparing to film, but Omar held up a firm hand, motioning for her to stop. The woman acted like we were acting from some kind of script that she thought she already understood. She wasn't aware of the electricity or uncertainty in the room because, to her, peace was some kind of Hollywood news ending that she kept persistently trying to capture.

"I ain't trying to be religious but I believe in the bible, and the bible says that the devil is the father of murder and I know that we are all the children of God," Omar said. "So the question is how have we been bamboozled, hoodwinked, and tricked into killing each other?" I had never heard Omar speak at that level—with that kind of force and magnetism. He was summoning his preacher father. "The devil has you beating, maiming, and killing one another," he went on. "The loser ends up dead or crippled, and the winner ends up with a life sentence. And six months later, no one remembers either of them."

I had never heard the game rationalized so bluntly. I queasily accepted it as truth; it looked as if others in the crowd were feeling the same way. He then asked, "Does anyone in here have a beef with someone else in either neighborhood that's worth fighting or dying for?"

A young Blood raised his hand. Omar pointed to him. The room held still, and the kid said, "My girl let me listen in on a three-way call and her friend lied on me about another girl I used to be with." The crowd erupted with a much-needed laugh. Even the reporter bent sideways from laughter. Omar was the only one trying to hold a straight face. He waited until the boisterous laughter subsided and then brought the room back into form.

"I understand your pain," he said, "but it's not a reason to fight, let alone contemplate taking another human life." For a few seconds, there was a surreal silence in the room. It was an amazing feeling to be in the midst of something like that—to feel the tremor of Omar's words pass across the crowd, to sense that change actually might be possible.

"There has been one revenge killing or shooting after another for the past fifteen years, with every excuse thinkable behind them," Omar went on. "But the truth is we have been the victims of lies and bankrupted of forgiveness. When someone offends you, violence and retribution is not the only option—we can *forgive*. Forgiving means to pardon before you punish. So instead of being eager to and ready to punish a perpetrator for every wrongdoing, let's try something new today, right this minute. Let's forgive what has happened and the misunderstood deeds that may happen tomorrow. Let's quit killing our brothers and sisters for wandering down the street or talking to a girl we like. Let's value their blood the way the mamas, grandmamas, fathers, grandfathers, and baby mamas value the blood that *they* have lost. They are tired of funerals, hospitals, and sons with life sentences 'cause ain't nobody winning but the devil. The OGs can make the call. Let's start a new tradition in South Dallas. Let's become a whole community rather than a divided neighborhood. Tonight, for the last few hours in our community, peace has been still. Let's make it last." This night reminded me of why I gave my life to helping to end the violence. I was proud.

Omar suggested, now that we'd all eaten and talked together, that we should pray together. As these guys had flowed into the room, the group had naturally divided based on colors—red and blue. Grover and I asked everybody to mix in for a moment of prayer; we urged everyone to move toward those in a different group and hold hands. There was enough positive energy still stirring in the room from Omar's talk that people were willing to do that, although not exactly comfortably. Then Omar led us in a fervent prayer. I still caught a whiff of skepticism in the crowd, but there was also an opening of some kind. People's facial expressions were more relaxed; it seemed like they had accepted what we were trying to do, even if they hadn't yet made their minds up.

"Can I get everyone close together for a photo?" the ABC World News reporter said, breaking in at just the wrong moment. I finally took the woman aside and told her that she wasn't going to get a photo-op, it was too delicate a time. She was visibly perturbed, but I was just happy she put her cameras away before somebody else got frustrated with her. People started filing out of the restaurant. Omar and the owner of Two Podners stayed back and gave the news reporter an interview. She may not have gotten the shot, or the happy ending, she'd been looking for—but in the real world, progress *had* been made. Two factions of the hardest youngsters had just sat and eaten together. Forging forgiveness.

18

Peace Be Still

Acouple of weeks after the peace summit, on August 12, 2000, Omar and I convened 170 gang members of both the 415 Bloods and 187 Park Row Crips in the Hall of State Building in Fair Park. We had convinced them all to sign a peace treaty—Omar and I had drawn up a formal document—to serve as the groundwork for our vision for the community. City leaders, police, clergy, schoolteachers, and the business community were also there to witness the event.

Grover and I joined Omar on stage. He led us in prayer and then turned to the community leaders and addressed them directly, forcefully stating that only parasites thrive in a war zone, eating the flesh of the dead and unburied victims of aggression. "We announce today the war that has crippled South Dallas is over," Omar told the crowd. "We seek to rebuild this historic community and revitalize its institutions." To invest in this community is to invest in its people, he continued, asking them to build their businesses as well as hire the members of our community as we ushered in a new era for a new generation. Grover and I spoke as well—each of us committing to peace in our own words—and the day ended with Omar reading the terms of the treaty, with the entire room reciting it back to him; afterwards, everyone lined up to sign it.

Within three months of my release from prison, I had taken part in a successful community intervention. It was unheard of: most people who commit to community activism don't so easily find their way, much less experience a clear sense of accomplishment. For me, it was both exhilarating *and* misleading. It fed my ambition—*activism*, at that point, meant that I could repeal the transgressions not only of my life but in the world too—while also allowing me to naively believe that change like this could be easily wrought.

Later that week, Omar and I met with Don Williams, the donor who'd made it possible for us to hold our peace summit at Fair Park, for lunch at a downtown restaurant. I had never met Don Williams in person, nor did I know how much Omar had already talked me up to him. But, after we sat down and got the small talk out of the way, he and Omar launched into a discussion about the possibility of my working full-time at Don's nonprofit, the Foundation for Community Empowerment. The conversation was flying by me, fast and furious. I felt like I was a spectator, sitting on the sidelines of my own job interview; the two of them were negotiating the terms of my position, what role I might play, what the salary would be (only slightly above minimum wage). The whole thing set me on edge.

Later, Omar would explain to me on a plane to Los Angeles that he'd been trying to get Don and me to meet not only because he knew that there would be a dynamic synergy between us but also because, at FCE, I would be able to continue the work I'd been doing with Vision Regeneration. After all, FCE was, in large part, one of the funding streams for Vision Regeneration. Working for Don would not only mean an increase in pay for me, along with benefits, it would also offer financial coverage for any education I might pursue. Omar was trying to put me on a path, one that would lead to a more stable life, while also allowing me to do the kind of work he felt I was clearly meant to do. But at that lunch, all I could see was that I was being pushed into new and unfamiliar territory without anyone consulting me.

Which is not to say that I wasn't excited about the possibility of a job with a higher salary. At that point, Vision Regeneration was only able to pay me a small amount of money for the work I was doing. I was passionate about it, which helped to keep me going, but it was tough to make ends meet—not to mention shift the expectations of my family, who still thought of me as the breadwinner no matter what or how many times I explained how my circumstances had changed.

Increasingly, though, my apprehension overtook my sense of opportunity while Don and Omar continued to deliberate over my future position and my skills. For one thing, I'd only ever had one real job before working with Omar—when I'd worked at the home health care service, more as a refuge than anything else, during the FBI crackdown in 1995. After that, I'd only been an actual employee at Vision Regeneration. But working with Omar hadn't actually felt like work at all; we were so aligned in sensibility and purpose it had simply felt like the natural next step in my life. I didn't know what being a "community liaison," as Don and Omar kept calling the position, entailed—or even if I could do it. Without Omar having yet explained to me that I would still be able to carry on my work at Vision Regeneration, I thought going to work for FCE meant leaving our original mission just as we were really starting to make a difference.

But, perhaps most importantly, I did not yet trust Don Williams.

Up to that point, when we needed resources or someone to commit funding to our plans, Omar had handled it. I really had no idea how he'd done it. I'd just carried on with our agenda, happy to have the financial backup or donation that we needed to keep moving forward. I hadn't realized how much was happening behind the scenes to keep money flowing in; I certainly never imagined that Omar had *another* partner in Don Williams, passionately scheming and strategizing with him just as I had been, about how to bring the neighborhoods of South Dallas forward into more harmonious communities.

When I'd been in prison and had first become immersed in my Malcolm X-inspired education, I became aware of how little I knew of Black history. It was a shock, honestly—before it was a motivation—to find how many people like me had come before; how many arms were reaching up from the past to lift me. So while I was reading books like *The Destruction of the Black Civilization: Great Issues of a Race from 4500 B.C. to 2000 A.D.* and *The Falsification of the Afrikan Consciousness: Eurocentric History, Psychiatry and Politics of White Supremacy*, I was not only deepening my historical perspective, I was also fanning my righteousness as I came to more substantially understand just how long, and how gruelingly, my people had been abused, dismissed, indoctrinated. This was also my earliest sense of wanting to participate in changing the course of history—really, this was my first commitment to activism—and it was based on my deepening intellect and pride. I was hungry to prove my point to anyone else who had somehow misunderstood or neglected to learn, as I had, just how deep the whip had cut. It made me reflect in a crucial and valuable way, but it also made me distrustful.

So on that day at lunch, even as my instincts told me that Don Williams was as passionate about keeping the peace in our community as I was, I couldn't stop from reflexively asking myself, *Why is this rich, white man so concerned with South Dallas—and me?*

But I was also always moving along two tracks in prison. That is, I was not only on a fanatical intellectual pursuit but I was also in the midst of spiritual transformation. And, at times, one would pull out in front of the other—my intellect would sharpen before my spirit and soul had fully opened, or the other way around. When this happened, particularly when my intellectual pride seemed to be over-taking my spiritual side, Fareed would occasionally intervene. Once, he pulled me aside and, seemingly out of nowhere, asked, "If you're trying to elevate a young brother, would you give him 1) a knowledge of self and history or 2) the knowledge of God?"

"Knowledge of self," I said immediately. "You've got to give a brother a sense of self and history, because, without that, he's doomed to repeat the past. We're in this position because we don't know who we are."

Fareed shook his head and put his hand on my shoulder. "If you give a person history first," he replied, "they can get stuck there, they can become bitter, angry, and suspicious. But if you give them the knowledge of God first, then they can connect to a larger pur-pose with passion and a vital sense of openness, thus able to process history."

I recalled this story on my walk home after my lunch with Omar and Don. At the time, I'd been surprised that Fareed had said my an-swer was wrong. My ego was still heavily wrapped up in my learning process and, as I answered, I felt certain, and proud, that I was saying the right thing. I'd felt that my righteous anger was the fire that lit it all up. I realized now though that what Fareed had advised was essential to the work I was trying to do with Omar—and apparently

Don Williams too. I couldn't have my own personal biases or rage or pride wrapped up in it; I had to operate with the commitment of my activism *and* the broad-mindedness of my faith.

When I got home that afternoon, the first thing I did was Google "J. McDonald Williams." I knew he was a real estate maverick, a philanthropist, and Dallas native but I was surprised to find that he was also a billionaire. He was controversial too; he had heavy supporters and detractors. But I knew enough by then to know that *everyone* has their supporters and detractors—not the least of which, white billionaires using their influence to affect change in predominantly Black neighborhoods. But I liked most of what I read—Don was outspoken, dynamic, and, as far as I could tell, on the right side of history. His unequivocal message was that there shouldn't be two Dallases: wealthy and poor; white and Black; tranquil and deadly. He felt that in order to have a great city, you needed an equal city— any other way wasn't moral, *and* it was bad for business. For nearly a decade, he had been on the front lines in southern Dallas, changing schools, gathering grant money to revitalize the neighborhoods, funding research. So why was this rich white man so concerned with South Dallas? It appeared that Don had what Fareed had been trying to fuse in me: passion and purpose. And if you've already got a billion dollars, I figured, it might not be about money, as some of Don's critics claimed; maybe he'd simply bought himself the time and space and power to tip the scales toward good in the world.

And so I decided to give Don a fair shot. It seemed to be the right step forward, not just toward a more stable job—though it would take a couple of years before it became official—but from a personal, sometimes judgmental, sense of activism to one that was larger than myself. Activism, I realized, was not only braided into my knowledge of God, it also offered its own kind of faith. I had to take myself out of the equation. I needed to judiciously accept others into my collaboration and community, understanding that, together, we would achieve so much more than I ever could on my own. It takes a village of everyone who genuinely cares to raise a child—well, that's true for a community too.

For me, Omar was not only a professional mentor—often strategically leaving, as he did that first meeting with Don, much for me to decipher and determine on my own—but he was also an intuitive spiritual guide, a deeply moral person, as considered as he was kind. And the depth of those qualities seemed to offer him an eerie, almost extrasensory, connection to what was going on with the people he was looking out for in the community.

One of the people Omar always carried in his heart was a teen who everybody called "Doo-Daddy." One bright fall day in October, Omar called me and said ominously, "Go find Doo-Daddy; he's in my spirit. I feel something is going on."

This was especially surprising to me because I hadn't actually seen Doo-Daddy—or thought about him—since before I'd gone to prison. My memories of him were as a young, goofy kid growing up across from me in Frazier Courts. He was always cracking jokes; he was the kind of kid you just started laughing with as soon as you got around him. His energy was just funny. In my mind, he was still an innocent eleven- or twelve-year-old boy with big saucer-like eyes, playing with my little brothers in the backyard under the clothesline in the projects. So to think that he was now grown enough to rep the Bloods, as Omar told me he'd done, or even that he might have gotten himself into trouble, seemed unnatural somehow.

Still, I went looking for him, as Omar had asked. I talked to people in the street, knocked on doors in Frazier Courts, asked around with the younger kids: "Anybody seen Doo-Daddy lately?" Nobody had, but they also weren't alarmed. Sometimes he went to a friend's house for days on end, they said, and anyways, news would have gotten around the neighborhood if something had happened.

The next day, I learned from a friend that Doo-Daddy had been murdered the day before, on his sixteenth birthday. Turned out, Doo-Daddy had wanted some money to spend on himself for his birthday and decided, with a friend, to burglarize a house. They kicked in the door, only to find that the house wasn't empty, as they'd thought, and they were met with gunfire. Apparently, Doo-Daddy's last words had been "play dead." He'd said this to his friend, lying next to him on the floor, so that the assailant would leave the scene believing he'd killed them both. After that, Doo-Daddy bled out. Doo-Daddy was such a beloved character in the community; the end of his life was felt as a personal tragedy by most everyone. It also seemed it might just be the deed that would undo the peace treaty.

The funeral was huge. The church was packed. It was a sea of red as every Blood in East Dallas turned out for this mournful loss. Omar delivered the eulogy. As Omar strode to the front of the church, to the shock of the crowd, Grover came in and viewed the casket, paying his respects as the head of the Crips. After Omar was finished speaking, Grover took the microphone and gave a heartfelt shout out to Doo-Daddy. That was unprecedented. I walked to the mic after Grover, surprising even myself by doing so, and thanked him for the remarkable gesture of showing up and sharing his memories about Doo-Daddy. "Revenge is more ruthless than even the way that our brother Doo-Daddy died. Back in the day, we didn't care what happened or why—all we wanted was for them to feel the pain we are feeling now," I said. "But I've changed, and now I am going to ask you to do what you have never thought about doing in this situation. Lay your flag down. This isn't about red and blue; this isn't about Crips and Bloods—it's about a game that nobody can win. We don't know why Doo-Daddy was killed, we can only speculate, but the leader of the Crips is here to say it's not a gang bangin' thang. It's a wrong thang." I walked back to my seat. I'd said what was in my heart. I didn't want another brother from any side to end up dead.

Amazingly, the peace held.

19

Each One, Teach One

There is a mystical tie between people who have evolved through life over a long period of time in the same community. But it is not only a cultural thing—people tending to share the same taste in food and clothes and music—it also creates a familial feeling, a sense that you are bonded by more than friendship, extending into the realm of mystery and light. There are disagreements, even knockdown fights, but there is also a genuine concern and hope for one another that I believe comes from the same emotional place where true activism is born.

From the start of our collaboration, Omar and I had been working on strategies that we could implement in the schools, allowing us to get in at the ground level and influence the new generation at a critical moment—as well as sustain the broader commitment to peace. I felt a personal connection to this effort because I knew we'd be working with kids like I had been—good kids under the powerful sway of the hood. Omar and I had merged our two proposals and added a twelve-week program we could bring into the schools. It included a course on benefits and consequences that Omar had taught at the Texas Youth Commission, plus conflict resolution workshops utilizing my skills drawn from my experience in prison facilitating conversations among gang members.

On the first morning of school, without an official contract, Omar and I decided to patrol the neighborhood to check that kids were actually going in. Near South Boulevard, we saw about forty youngsters hanging out, laughing and messing around. We stopped and asked them why they weren't in school.

"The principal kicked us out," one of them answered defiantly. "We tried to get started at Madison, but the principal told us we had to leave. Our very first day—we ain't even had a chance to do anything yet and he told us to leave."

I flashed back to my own first day at Madison, when the principal marched over to my friends and me—calling each of us out by our street names to show he had our numbers—and then warned us we'd be suspended if we caused any trouble. It had been an inauspicious beginning to an inauspicious year. I felt for these youngsters, who were so full of life but clearly felt as dejected as I had when the principal had done that, grinding what little hope I had for the school year to dust and blowing it back at me from the palm of his hand. The biggest misunderstandings of my young life occurred when adults took my swagger at face value. Most of the time, I felt more terrified over all the things I had to encounter to simply exist than tough. It seems obvious to me now—but time and again, I see adults recoil in fear from *children* who have simply put on a brave face in a crushingly rough world. I reflected back to the prison of all the guys I had met along the way, who were angry, tattoos adorning their entire bodies, grimacing look on the outside, but on the inside they were afraid little boys, unsure of how to ask for help.

Omar and I headed over to Madison to talk to the principal, Mr. Ward, on behalf of these kids. We'd decided to volunteer our services, offering to patrol the school if Mr. Ward would allow them back in. We knew that if we didn't make a bold effort, those young men would probably never go to the alternative school and their prospects for graduation would be over. They'd be left to hang out on the streets and get into trouble, starting the cycle over again. To our amazement, Mr. Ward agreed to our unusual proposal. The next day, along with Omar, our small crew and I were roaming the corridors of my old school doing intervention and prevention. We brought in some neighboring OGs.

Omar and I knew that just seeing us walking the halls of the school would work, on some level, as a kind of cognitive intervention. That is, just by being there, we, an OG and the son of a gangster-turned-preacher, were saying to them, "School is the way." This, in combination with the curriculum we'd devised, helped to make our approach cutting edge and innovative. Nobody had ever challenged gang culture in Dallas—it had simply been a rite of passage—but now Omar and I were starting a new conversation.

From the start, we found ourselves returning again and again to in-school suspension, where the kids who'd been late, unruly, confrontational, or otherwise disruptive were held. Back then, those kids were put in a room and left alone with a book until further notice—as if they were suddenly going to sit quietly and read. Omar and I quickly realized we could take advantage of that time to get to know the students and talk about their lives. Their problems ranged from being hungry—most hadn't eaten before coming to school and so had a bad attitude from the get-go—to not being able to afford a belt to keep their pants up to feeling serious confusion and rage because one of their parents was in prison. Once we felt the kids trusted us, we began to teach them conflict resolution techniques, impulse control, empathy for others, respect for authority. We were doing the work that other administrators felt was too challenging, or time consuming, to deal with in-house. Sometimes the solution was as simple as listening to the kids without flinching or worrying they'd do something rash. Some of them were massive, a red bandana or shirt to identify them as one of the Bloods, and they talked a big game. But when Omar or I gave them ten minutes of undivided attention, it was possible to see past that. It was possible even to see *inside* that; I swear I sometimes caught a glimpse of the six-year-old boy frozen in time within the grown-too-soon layers of these young men. I could relate because I was once those kids. They understood.

During the first sixty days of school, there wasn't a single gang fight. There wasn't a shooting, no one was hurt, and the exclusionary discipline procedures that had ultimately landed so many of the kids in alternative schools were being employed at the lowest rate seen in a year. There was no denying it: within a couple of months, we were getting results in a school that had been in crisis for years—further back than even I could remember.

It wasn't an easy ride, of course. To gain our footing took patience and learning from our mistakes along the way. There was also a certain amount of ribbing. Some of the active gang members at the school would call out things at us in the hallways, like: "How can the blind lead the blind?" and "Where did you get your degree from, Rob, Steal, and Bang?" But the biggest surprise for me was the enduring suspicion of the school security and a good number of teachers and administrators. I'd naively thought that everyone would be happy with the help we were offering, and, when that didn't happen, I'd mistakenly hoped that, after the results were clearly positive, they'd begin to value our efforts. But at every turn, it seemed, we only incited our detractors more. They would brush us off in the hallways, say unkind things behind our backs, and undermine the work we were doing by denying that anything positive was happening. Finally, I decided that their contempt, at least in part, sprang from prejudice and professional jealousy. The majority of our detractors looked like us. They couldn't believe that ex-gang members with no formal education were able to bring order when they'd spent the better part of their careers unsuccessfully trying to wrangle the kids into shape. This revelation—that people could be so small-minded as to get in the way of beneficial progress—really woke me up. I'd been living in a fairy tale until then, believing that help was help and everybody could and would appreciate it when it was offered.

Luckily, the principal at Madison came to believe in those kids first and foremost, and he also believed in our methodology. The superintendent gave us a contract to continue our work, and we ended up being referred to also bring the same approach to Lincoln High School. Those achievements—not only that we made measurable progress but also that our work was legitimized in this way—kept us going.

And yet I couldn't stop thinking about Doo-Daddy's death and the fact that we still hadn't put together outreach for people like him—young kids not in school but on the streets, attracted to fast money and criminal lifestyles. I knew that whatever force had pulled Doo-Daddy toward gang life and burglarizing and drugs—and finally to his early death—was continuing to draw other vulnerable kids too. It was the same force that had arrested me.

Truthfully, they were the ones who needed the most help but

were the least targeted for outreach. They operated in red light districts high in crime and police presence. The sad, stark reality was that outreach for kids dealing drugs didn't yield as high a turnover as advocating for peace with gang youth or reducing dropouts in school. As a result, there was little money available to activist organizations for the kind of work needed to make a difference. Since I was able to move through those familiar streets with ease because of my history, I thought I could take it on without as many challenges. I knew the ins and outs of that world, how to handle the players and dealers. And I didn't fear the police any longer—I was on the right side of things, trying to get those kids *out* of the game rather than get back in it myself. And I was firmly committed to the proverb and principle "each one, teach one," to which I would add, "then reach back and get one—until everybody has been saved."

Unfortunately, the police didn't see things the same way. After a while, I started hearing rumors from friends that the police were asking about me when they arrested other people in the neighborhood, trying to get information about what I was up to. Apparently, they were claiming that I was dealing again and "acting like an activist" as a cover. So while I was out in the community talking to the kids who were in trouble, they put me under surveillance, waiting for the day I would slip up and they could arrest me again.

20

GANG BUSTERS

The *Dallas News* ran a front-page story about us, along with photos of Omar and me, calling us "Gang Busters," citing the progressive efforts we'd been making in the schools. It was nice to be recognized publicly for all the usual reasons—I felt appreciated, vindicated, and I can't say that it didn't stoke the flames of my ego a bit too—but my most gratifying reaction was a subconscious one. Somehow the recognition permitted me to shed some of the defensiveness I'd built up around the poor reception we'd gotten from the faculty in the schools, as well as the negative stance the police had taken toward me. I hadn't yet realized that this would forever be an internal tug of war—between trying to do the right thing and letting go of virtuous indignation toward those that didn't accept my actions as such. In a way, it was the most satisfied I'd ever feel because at this early stage in the game, I believed I'd actually managed to fully let go of the embittered feelings that can unexpectedly and uncomfortably ride alongside activism.

That summer, Omar and I decided we would host a camp program. We had three major initiatives. One, continue the peace that was still holding; two, change the history of summer conflicts by creating a program that would bring kids together, off the streets, for food and fun; three, prepare our youth to re-enter school without an expectation of violence. The summer months were where the surge in violence happened.

While we had started out as a gang program, the reality was that we were dealing with kids with issues that stretched far beyond. Many of them were experiencing an identity crisis similar to the one I'd felt as a kid. They had become so inured to crime and violence they didn't realize that they were being rolled along the same conveyor belt as everyone else around them; there was no explicit message, no loud-speaker announcing, "*You* are next. You might only be stealing today, but you could kill an innocent person tomorrow. Fighting over that girl could lead to a stabbing. Staying out late at night can open you up to being shot." They didn't think like that because nobody thinks like that in the hood. Everybody is too busy surviving; there isn't a chance to step back, catch your breath, and look at it from a distance.

We created our summer program as a way to address these young people and their families. We wanted to be more vocal and more explicit about the blunt realities of living in a high-crime area. We needed to tell our kids what many parents felt they already knew, though since they couldn't see any solutions they were just trying to block it out. Meanwhile, unable to talk about their fears or even to buy decent clothes, with no positive affirmations, the kids often acted out the most in the summer when they had few to no restraints.

We arranged to run the day camp in Faith Memorial Church, where Omar and I were working out of as our office. We had enough funding to hire a few teachers; some volunteers came in to offer spe-cialized courses, such as painting and theater, as well as a food pro-gram that donated meals.

The demand was overwhelming. We expected seventy-five kids, at most—but on the first day, two hundred kids showed up. They were hungry and rowdy; most of them seemed to be overcompensating with pride and saunter, acting clownish or excessively tough while clearly feeling a steady undercurrent of powerlessness. These kids were so numb to their environment, with many of their parents distracted by their own overwhelming lives, they simply needed someone to pay attention to their lives and show them that what they thought and did mattered; they needed someone to make them feel visible.

In the end, I felt that, while we were able to minimize what could have been worse, we weren't able to reach and rescue as many youth as we'd hoped with the program. We could've done more if there had been twenty, thirty, fifty, or a hundred of us. But only Omar, Grover, Big Rick, K-Ray, Cook, Chew, and I were doing the intervention work, along with the help of the small staff of counselors we'd managed to put together. It was frustrating, and humbling, to see the numbers of kids seeking our help and then to feel, in the end, we'd only been able to meet them halfway. I still felt an enormous rush of pride and accomplishment at the summer program graduation, but, from then on, I have also carried with me a cautious awareness that I will not take on more than I can handle.

In the fall of 2001, after we'd gone back to work in the schools, Omar and I were invited to a conference in Washington, DC, by one of his mentors, Bob Woodson, the head of an organization called the National Center for Neighborhood Enterprise. This organization, now known as the Woodson Center, recognizes, trains, and funds community-based leaders; it was hosting the conference What Works and Why, meant to explore community building and how to stop violence in low-income communities. I was looking forward to meeting

Bob, who Omar clearly admired; I was also curious to talk to people from all over the country doing work similar to ours. Overall, the invitation also seemed like a good sign that we were doing things right.

When we arrived at the conference, I had a chance to see Bob Woodson speak. He was not what I expected. I knew that he was African American and that he was a powerful civil rights activist who'd been working faithfully in the world of community building for over forty years. He'd directed community development programs for the NAACP; he'd been a social worker with the Unitarian Services Committee; as a director at the National Urban League, he'd spearheaded neighborhood empowerment programs, and he'd gone on to lead the American Enterprise Institute's Neighborhood Revitalization Project in Washington, DC. I knew, and respected, that Omar and I stood on the shoulders of many giants—and a sturdy pair of them belonged to Bob Woodson.

What I did not know, however, was that Bob Woodson was a Republican. I have not always been a political observer. Until that point, I had basically thought about politics in broad strokes—and one of those strokes was that Republicans were white. In the arena of community building, I'd mostly encountered Democrats; in that world, Republicans were more often demonized—they were venal, they didn't care about the little guy, they weren't civic-minded, and, even if this last idea was left largely unexpressed, they were *not* Black. So when Bob took the podium and spoke forthrightly, brashly at times, expressing his views on structural racism and the ways in which it was used not to reveal the problems of lower-income Black neighborhoods but rather to *deflect* them, I was taken aback. Accusations of racism, he said, took away attention from the failures of the politicians and people running the institutions meant to help. In the past fifty years, the

U.S. had spent 20 trillion dollars fighting a war on poverty and it had barely moved the needle. And 70 percent of that 20 trillion, he went on, had been spent on the bureaucracies that dispensed the money to organizations that serve poor people. But the real solution to poverty, Bob explained, can be found among the people who are actually suffering from it. At his organization, they examined the 30 percent of low-income families achieving against the odds and then figured out what *they* were doing in order to teach it to others. It is not about exemptions or reparations, he declared. We must face the hurdles with enough tenacity and fervor to get over them, and we must quit waiting for the government to do for us what we can do for ourselves *now*.

Woodson was clearly unconcerned about what others might make of his exceptional opinions—and he came across like a powerhouse. As far as I could tell, his conviction had set him free from *any* constraints, political or otherwise. He had the expertise, experience, and knowledge to be a true progressive—that is, he was tackling a social issue, reasoning out the best way to act on it, and then advocating for a way to reform. He didn't seem to care who was Democrat or Republican, or Black or white. He was more practical than that, and blunter; he forcefully wanted change. He had been such an electrifying speaker—he'd actually conjured Frederick Douglass for me. "I would unite with anybody to do right," I remembered Douglass once saying, "and with nobody to do wrong."

I didn't agree with everything that Bob said—I still think he can get in his own way, given the extremes to which he'll go to prove his point—but I learned to take from his argument what I needed in order to shape my own opinion. In time, as I got to know him better, I also learned that debating Bob about how to revitalize communities or combat poverty or understand racism was an education unto itself. I'd sharpen my own views against the steel of Bob's beliefs, and I always came out the other side, if a little battered, better acquainted with my own mind.

In the end, the lesson, for me, was not just realizing that a Black man could indeed be a conservative, but that progressive activism exists in a realm beyond politics. Conversations—in which people with differing views actually hear each other—and action based on an understanding wrought from those difficult exchanges are the driving forces of activism; without them, we're just running in place. So even when Bob is bombastic, declaring "he doesn't know what systemic racism is," as he once did on Fox news, I can also hear that he is saying that we need to focus more on what we should demand from the politicians and institutions that have not yet succeeded in pulling our people out of poverty. And that many of those living in poverty have already done an exceptional job of bringing themselves up on their own—we should be paying attention to what they have to teach us.

Having once hated every Crip to the point that I wouldn't even say a word with the letter C in it, to the point where I was shooting at people over a turf war I didn't really understand, to the point where I watched kids die before they'd even had a chance to glimpse the promise of their own lives—and then, after it all, to look deep down into my hatred, only to find nothing there—has given me an explicit perspective on the intractable differences between political parties in this country. People can become so dug into their positions, they stop listening altogether; they stop being able to think outside the box, outside of themselves. But if I could put down my gun and work with Grover to end gang violence, I sure as hell could see past politics to collaborate with Bob Woodson on making real change in urban communities.

21

***

A New Perspective

I, Antong Glenn Lucky, a.k.a. Kiddo—first arrested at age thirteen, in prison by age twenty-one, now barely twenty-five—was chosen to be mayor of Dallas for a day. Ron Kirk was the first African American mayor of Dallas. He'd won the mayor's race with 62 percent of the votes in 1995 and then was re-elected with a whopping 74 percent. He was beloved in the African American community and also had a great deal of white support. To mark the occasion, which had occurred almost two years to the day since I'd walked out of jail, I wrote Fareed a long letter about the changes that I had made since I met him—in large part *because* of him.

The morning I was meant to meet the mayor and take on his role for the day, I had butterflies in my stomach. I kept thinking that I might freeze in the midst of it all, just as I had a few years back in prison in my first speech to the prisoners. What if I didn't know what to say? What if I didn't know how to act? My whole life, I'd been winging it—first as a gang leader and now as an activist; the idea of showing up in a professional setting without any idea of what I was supposed to do was terrifying. But when I walked into Mayor Ron

Kirk's office, he stood, shook my hand, looked me in the eyes, and genuinely told me how proud he was of the work I'd been doing in South Dallas. And it was just us—no cameras, pretentions, or people to impress—so I was able to relax into the situation.

Mayor Kirk asked if I was ready to run the city.

"I am, sir," I said.

The mayor shared his daily briefing and told me the hot-button issues, preparing me for the city council meeting I would take part in that day. We talked about the construction of the 236-million-dollar sports arena and how he was getting flak from the inner city for not putting more money into its revitalization. At the city council meeting, we sat next to each other, and he introduced me to the council members. I briefly spoke about the work Omar and I had been doing and the incredible experiences we'd had, along with the positive statistics and research coming out of the schools we were working in. They gave me a round of applause, and then began the business of the city.

Mayor Kirk and I spent the day talking about the need to be inclusive, that urban America was changing and would never again be controlled by a one-race majority but by leaders who had the wisdom to unite people based on the principles of our democracy. He told me civility and patriotism were the core causes of unity in our city; if I promoted them, I would attract people who wanted to help solve the problems that were stifling our growth.

The people I was meeting and experiences I was having along my path after prison felt like steppingstones, each one moving me a bit closer to a philosophy of activism all my own. Along those lines, in 2002, I moved into Eban Village, a relatively new development in Park Row, in Crip territory. The year prior, I had been asked to become a community resident board member for Southfair Community Development Corporation, whose mission is to improve the quality of life for residents of South Dallas by creating affordable housing and offering homeownership counseling and services. It sounded as if it would be nice, and, at last, I could afford it. From a professional perspective, I believed it would help to create a broader community, further bringing the Crips and Bloods together, and would set the example of living together peaceably that I wanted others to follow.

From a personal perspective, too, it felt like a new start. By then, my relationship with Kesha had taken an unexpected turn. I'd been so focused on rebuilding my life when I first got out of jail—building my partnership with Omar, struggling to make ends meet, focusing on the peace treaty and the work that came after it—it had inadvertently taken a toll on my time with Kesha. She felt, understandably, that I didn't have much left at the end of the day for our relationship. From my perspective, the transformation I was undergoing, invisible as it was to other people, meant everything to me—but I couldn't figure out quite how to put that into words at the time. Eventually, Kesha exploded with the resentment she'd been bottling up and we began to argue. Ultimately, I felt it was only fair for me to move out; I thought she'd be better off finding someone who wasn't still in mid-flight, as I was. Not even a month after we'd broken up, however, Kesha learned she was pregnant. It felt as if I couldn't get this one piece of my life right, that my cross to bear was always somehow being removed from my children. When our son, Amir Antong Lucky, was born, healthy and handsome, on April 2, 2001, I vowed that I would make the same effort I'd been making with Tileyah, now four years old. I had worked double time to make up for what had been stolen from her by my being in prison, but I knew in my heart that I would never be able to excuse that trauma fully. Now I devoted every spare moment to spending time with both of my children, hoping they would never feel the paternal absence that had blighted my own childhood.

Soon after I'd moved to Eban Village, Bob Woodson, recognizing the work that Omar and I had done in the schools in Dallas as a success, asked if we'd be willing to assist in conceptualizing the violence-free zone across the country. He called this program the violence-free zone initiative and helped connect us to donors to help fund it. Omar and I had grown our staff to twenty people while working at Madison and Lincoln in Dallas, bringing in other OGs like Cook, DoDoo, and Grover, to help monitor the schools, mediate conflict, and act as mentors. Bob believed we could scale our operation up to the next level. The next thing I knew, we were flying to different conferences across the country, training participants to do what we were doing. For a while, I was traveling so much I was only home in Dallas for a couple of days a week before I was off to the West or East Coast for another training session or meeting. We were talking with city council members, community activists, sociologists, law enforcement officers. Our techniques worked across the board, and we quickly gained visibility and recognition within the realm of the nonprofit community.

Then, one evening, traveling back to Dallas from Baltimore, Omar asked me how far was I willing to travel to teach these principles. I thought he was joking so I laughed and said, "To the ends of the earth."

"What about Russia?" he asked.

I couldn't quite figure out where the conversation was going. My mind searched for something I knew about Russia. The only thing

I could come up with was the image of Ivan Drago, the big Russian character who fights Apollo Creed and kills him in the *Rocky* movie—and then Rocky has to almost die to beat him in revenge. Omar explained that the Bradley Foundation, a conservative charitable organization, had asked Bob to train the leaders at nongovernment organizations (NGOs) on how to tackle youth violence; Bob had recommended us for the job. I was floored. Until we'd started working with Bob, I'd barely traveled around the U.S., much less been out of the country. When I got home, I immediately called my parole officer and said, "I need a passport and approval to leave the country. I'm headed to St. Petersburg, Russia."

The flight lasted eighteen hours. I felt nervous from the moment I stepped on the plane. I was shocked when everybody around me fell asleep as we rocketed through the air. My mind was revving—how long I was going to be stuck on this airplane, what would Russia be like? I strategized about how we were going to relate our stories to the NGO workers and whether our ideological approach would be replicable in a foreign setting. When we landed, I experienced an entirely new and separate sense of culture shock. The architecture, signs, colors, language, and people—all of it was exotic to me.

Our interpreter was a big Russian guy named Sasha, who, at first sight, was as mean-looking as Ivan Drago—but over time, he proved himself to be a stand-up guy. He instructed us to stay within the security zone of the five-star hotel we were staying in. I realized the next day why he'd offered that warning so forcefully when a guide took us through what was basically the Frazier Courts of Russia. At that time, the country was only a decade or so past communist rule. The youth were hungry for material wealth, which had coincided with a proliferation of gangs—and all the problems that go along with them.

The neighborhoods were run down, the streets rough; kids were victims both of gang violence and the Russian mafia.

When we first met with some of the gang members, speaking through a translator, they seemed cold. I tried telling them about my own upbringing in Frazier Courts, drug trafficking, gun charges, and the juvenile boys' home. I mostly got blank stares or, worse, sideways glances and sighs of disinterest. Then I showed them my bullet wound—and the conversation was on. These kids were *tough*. But once I broke through, we had a meaningful conversation about the realities of the streets.

What really stayed with me was how few Black people there were in Russia. Most of the Black youth, it seemed, were foreign exchange students from Africa, France, and Britain. I didn't see a single Black person just walking around until I went to a jazz club in St. Petersburg—he was the guy in the bathroom selling cologne. I was thrilled to see him, to find someone I might be able to talk to about the culture of Russia through the lens of being Black. I patted him on the back and said, "What's up, bro?!" He looked at me quizzically—and I remembered that he probably didn't speak English.

It was so unusual to see an American Black person in the streets, in fact, that sometimes as we were walking the city, cars pulled over and people jumped out to take our picture. Somehow, they always knew we were American, and they assumed we were rich. They treated us like we were Michael Jordan or Denzel Washington. I realized, later, that they were likely the only Black people they knew about—the celebrities they saw on TV. I recalled, too, that the jazz club we'd visited was lined with framed photographs of great Black musicians—Ella Fitzgerald, Louis Armstrong, and Miles Davis. Russia clearly has enormous and profound problems, and racism ranks among them, but in my brief experience, it was startling to encounter this *other* narrative, or set of preconceived notions, about Black people.

On one of our last days, we visited a Russian prison, which left an indelible impression. It made Beto One look like the five-star hotels we were staying in during our tour of Russia. There were no televisions, tables, or hot water. The cells were filthy and the whole place smelled like old cabbage. The inmates looked as if they were starving to death, their bodies lined with bruises. Each one was either freshly beaten or overworked. They were quiet and stoic and they stared at us as we walked past them with such raw looks of despair, I almost had to look away when our eyes locked. I *knew* how bleak it was for them. Though their experience looked as if it were more torturous than mine, it didn't take much for me to imagine what it would be like to be locked up in such an inhumane place day after day after day.

The trip to Russia helped me begin to form a world view. Being on an international stage and collaborating with another group of social activists committed to the welfare of people in their country nudged me to widen the lens on my activism—to see beyond racial inequality toward incorporating the universal burden of socioeconomic disparity. In the hard faces of those young gang members and the afflicted expressions of the prisoners, I had found a common sense of desperation and an immediate need for help. On the plane back to the United States, I was glad to be American in America.

22

THE AUDACITY OF ACTIVISM

By 2005, I had officially begun working for Don Williams's Foundation for Community Empowerment in the role of community liaison that Omar and Don had first hammered out long ago. In working for him, I'd come to know Don better in a way that made me grateful for resisting my early skeptical instincts. In my first few months at FCE, though, my antennae were still very much up: I was anxious and ready to serve my community. I paid very close attention to the organization and the work I was being asked to do—always scanning for evidence that Don was just "another rich white guy trying to take over the neighborhood," as some of my friends and colleagues warned me. The conclusion I came to instead was that Don sincerely cared about the community. After working for some time with him up close and personal, I understood that Don Williams was building his legacy, and a big part of that included providing equity for underserved parts of Dallas.

As promised, I was still working closely with Omar at Vision Regeneration, but we were also making efforts to revitalize areas alongside Don. Our main objective was to develop South Dallas into an attractive neighborhood where families thrived and children were safe. At the time, the community was blighted with abandoned houses, broken glass, condoms on the sidewalks, syringes in parks, and unpainted, crumbling store fronts; all the signs of a neighborhood unable to attract new investments.

This was a project near and dear to my heart, not only because I, too, lived in South Dallas but also because of the time I'd spent in suburban Desoto immediately after I'd gotten out of prison. Desoto is a beautifully maintained neighborhood that readily shows the pride and care its residents take in it. The lawns are manicured and symmetric; the grass is vibrant green; the houses are inviting. I realized how important this was to a person's mental health when as soon as I entered South Dallas every time I went to work I immediately felt as if my battery were drained. And the reverse would happen on my way home: when I crossed the line into Desoto, I was lifted up and my mind immediately felt open and freer. I came to understand more broadly that the look and feel of our communities has a profound effect on the collective mental state of the people living there.

Don put me in charge of a project he called the Slumlord Initiative. I looked into the slumlords of South Dallas and learned that they owned most of the dilapidated houses and burned-down lots in the area—and the ones that they didn't own were often those that had been left behind when someone died without a will and were stalled in probate court. My research also showed that 72 percent of the residents in South Dallas were renters. I spent months talking to elderly residents who lived next to these blighted, abandoned houses, frequented by drug users and sex workers, as well as homeless people who fervently prayed for a solution to the problem. But we kept hitting a wall in terms of how we could intervene, until Don Williams' struck upon an idea—a terrific but tricky idea.

In the seventies, when South Dallas was a thriving, middle-class African American community with 76,000 residents, the city of Dallas used a legal maneuver called eminent domain—which exercises the power of the government to take private property and convert it to public use for just compensation (essentially the market value of the house, but, as always with real estate, "just compensation" is a complex notion)—to snatch homes from elderly Black homeowners in order to create a parking lot that would accommodate white patrons who came flocking to the annual State Fair in October. That incident left a lingering, terrible feeling among Black people—and a shuddering hatred of the term *eminent domain.*

And therein was the rub: Don Williams' proposal was to use a limited form of eminent domain to claim these absentee properties. He meant for it to only be used in cases where there were either no clear owners or where the probate court couldn't locate clear owners. Then the community development (CHDOs) would buy each property for one dollar from the city. In return, the CHDO would turn them into affordable housing for residents to buy or rent. Don was clear from the outset that he didn't want this to affect any homeowners, that this initiative would only claim properties with absentee landlords. I thought it was a win-win, a progressive way to deal with an old problem that had plagued the community for the past two decades.

As word of the plan spread, though, older activists, who'd cut their teeth during the Civil Rights era, began referring to Omar and me as "the dupes of Don Williams." They called Don a carpetbagger—reported in the Dallas morning newspaper—and claimed that he had sinister motives and a hidden plan to steal all the vacant lots in South Dallas. They didn't offer a reason for *why* he'd want to do this—they just somehow knew that this guy had bad intentions. Meanwhile, many of the activists who were speaking out had long ago moved out of South Dallas to live in the suburbs. In fact, by that time, 72 percent of the buildings in South Dallas were owned by white slumlords.

We planned a community meeting to discuss the issue at the Juanita Craft Recreation Center. When we—Omar, the director of the FCE, and myself (Don Williams sat that one out, given the controversy surrounding it)—arrived, we found it was standing room only. Over five hundred people were in attendance. As I waited to go in, I recognized a lot of local politicians milling about; they were all people I'd become familiar with, and admired, as I'd come into consciousness as an activist after I'd left prison. One of them walked up to me—an older, elegant African American female in a business suit, a local politician I'd understood to be a strong community advocate. My hopes were raised a little in anticipation of meeting her. I thought at least I'd have a chance to explain my point of view. Instead, she rolled her eyes as she approached and, pointing a finger at me, spat out under her breath, "Look here, motherfucker, you better not be selling your people out to these white folks."

And then she turned and walked away.

I was reeling. I knew there was controversy brewing, but I was still green enough to think the meeting was going to be a dialogue about our differences; I had no idea that it was basically an indictment— and we'd already been found guilty. And then a disturbing thought darted across my mind: *Am I on the right team?*

Moments later, the director of the FCE took to the podium.

Before he'd got even two words out, the audience erupted. They started booing and yelled for him to "sit his Uncle Tom ass down." I thought about South Dallas, condom wrappers and drug paraphernalia littering its streets; I thought about walking kids to school, as I had done over the years, through that garbage; I thought about the people who actually lived in the neighborhood, including myself, and the damage the blight was doing to our community. I shook off the comment from the female politician—and my confidence came roaring back, along with a sense of fury. The director was still trying to get a word in edgewise as the audience berated him. I walked up, grabbed the microphone, and asked the crowd of politicians, community activists, and lawmakers, "What is *your* plan? How do you want to change this community from its current look into something beautiful? Have you even read the plan? Don Williams won't win if we do this, *we* will win. If you disagree, then please come up and tell me about your plan for a different way forward for South Dallas."

The crowd quieted down. I spoke some more about our proposal to use a limited form of eminent domain for good—not in the historical understanding and context of the term. I could see that the audience was showing me respect—maybe partly out of fear, because they all knew I'd started the Bloods in Dallas. Whatever it was, it was fortunate for all of us, because I was ready to take them on with the same hostility and aggression they'd shown us. Still, even as they showed me cautious consideration, it was clear that I was not changing their minds. They stood firm on the fact that eminent domain was a nonstarter. For me, leaving the neighborhood in its current state was reckless and irresponsible, an expression of civil impotence that rattled every bone in my body. How could we progress if we continued to do the same thing, refusing to even hear a new thought or idea? Without conversation or debate, there was no chance that we'd find a place where we might come together. At the same time, I knew that if it were five years earlier, I likely would have joined those standing in knee-jerk opposition to us; I, too, wouldn't have been able to see past my own inchoate sense of injustice and the provocative phrase *eminent domain*. I'd had the great advantage of developing a sense of strategic activism, which, along the way, had opened my thought process, not only allowing me to see things from fresh angles but also offering a feeling of possibility for the future that many of these people seemed to have long forgotten.

What I saw in the eyes of the politicians and activists in the audience that night as I spoke—even after I'd commanded their attention—was dismissal, as though *I* didn't understand the game. And, in turn, that changed the way I saw them. It opened my eyes to a realm of activism that exists in name only; the air had been so thoroughly let out of these people's hopes, they were simply going through the motions. They weren't interested in thinking about things differently or receiving someone outside of their tightknit circle. But there was still another, even more depraved, reason these people saw Don, Omar, and me as trespassers on their community: it was a pay-to-play scheme. That is, among those politicians and activists, there was an implicit understanding that you've got to pay a toll to come into their neighborhood. The people in charge wouldn't allow change in the neighborhood until you put some change in their pockets. Meanwhile, they continue to bitterly question, looking askance at anyone who tried to help, why the neighborhood remained in decay. In fact, over the next decade several people who were at the meeting that night—including the female politician who'd hissed at me before I went on stage—ended up in federal prison for tax fraud, accepting bribes, and shaking down affordable-housing developers who'd dared enter their territory to try to make it a better place.

I prayed after that meeting. I asked God if I was on the right path. I questioned whether I wanted to continue in the face of the corruption existing at the very heart of our efforts. But what they saw as naive in me that night, I came to realize, was actually my defining force—an authentic and optimistic commitment to the community—and from that point forward it became the well from which I would drink when I felt my resolve drying up.

23

<hr>

VISION REGENERATION

In 2006, the national conversation about the school-to-prison pipeline, in which disadvantaged, predominantly Black students were
shunted into the criminal justice system for misbehaving at school,
was relatively new. The story, however, was an old one. Having once
myself been a teenager suspended from school, then held in the juvenile department and sent to state school, only to subsequently end up
in prison, I knew well the realities of the pipeline. So when, after six
years of Vision Regeneration leading initiatives for peace in schools,
we were approached to expand our services to include the Dallas
County Juvenile Department, which houses seven thousand kids between the ages of ten and seventeen, I saw an incredible opportunity.
I had a firm grasp on the issue, personally and professionally, and I
knew that the endeavor would place us squarely at the intersection of
the past, present, and future leaders of our urban community.

The contract we were given stated that we would be able to work
with these kids—all of whom identified as gang related—for 120
days, at which point they'd be on their own to assimilate to life after
juvie. So we got to work creating a specific agenda to prevent young

people from reoffending and to help them consciously make the choice to denounce gangs once they were back at home. We brought in NFL legend Deion "Prime Time" Sanders—whom we'd recruited the year prior to be the keynote speaker at our Solutions Conference, which was our second peace treaty—as well as Don Williams and two giants in the field of education, Dr. Allen Sullivan and the late Dr. H.B. Bell. Drs. Sullivan and Bell, both of whom I was referred to years ago when I was kicked out of Madison High School—both respected civil rights advocates with superior experience pioneering programs in the Dallas Independent School District to ensure children of color succeed—were on hand to discuss how we could implement the latest evidence-based gang interventions and preventions. We also intentionally hired young college students along with redeemed felons to help administer and facilitate the programs. (When Omar spoke about our model, he would sometimes joke that Vision Regeneration had more convicted felons on staff than some crime families employ.) And Omar's father, Reverend Jefferson, allowed us to use his church, Faith Memorial COGIC, as our home base for the program.

Soon after, we also put together a team of volunteers comprised of prominent business leaders to work with the kids. Omar and I knew how important it was for our teens to form relationships with a wide range of people, as well as for these businessmen and women to come to truly know and understand our teens.

And, lastly, a year into the program, I took a pay cut in order to have the great honor of adding my prison mentor and brother Fareed to our staff. I knew his intuitive understanding of the youth we were serving would make all the difference. And he had a personal story, and mission, that kept him firmly committed: As an orphan, he'd also gone through the juvenile system as a teen; now, in his mid-forties, he was helping solve problems that had plagued him for most of his life for these children. He became a teacher and big brother in the program. With him on board, I was able to shift from facilitation of the classes to focusing on one-on-one daily counseling. Fareed also introduced the notion that "a lot of love cures a lack of love," pointing out that many of these kids' problems sprang from a deficiency of emotional support in the family. If we wanted to reach these kids within our allotted 120 days, he pointed out, we needed to show them an abundance of love immediately.

We embraced the concept and trained our team to focus on the kids' feelings, pain, and loss rather than on immediate compliance with rules and regulations. We modeled affirmative language and instructed them to listen carefully for the youth's emotional needs. Essentially, we brought social and emotional learning into our program, which made a critical difference; it became our "secret sauce."

On Tuesday nights, we offered a spiritual component to our program that we dubbed Tuesday Night Hype. Though it was really bible study for the youth, we got creative about the way we framed it so the kids would not reject it outright. Some of the youth had expressed antichurch sentiments, and, generally speaking, kids are far more likely to get excited about a hype night than a bible study class. This was our way of introducing, or, for some, reintroducing, the concept of spirituality we felt these kids needed to feel supported and stable going forward. Eventually, we combined the Tuesday Night Hype group with students from Park Row, Frazier Courts, and another South Dallas neighborhood called Bonton. Ultimately it widened into an urban inner city prayer service.

A lot of great kids came through the program and benefited

immensely from it. Neko, for instance, was a young man on probation for bringing a gun to school. Despite his momentary lapse in
judgment, Neko was a smart kid with a great character. We connected him with one of our business-leader volunteers, and they developed a good friendship. Neko, who was in high school, told his
mentor that he was aiming to be the first in his family to attend college. Impressed, the volunteer offered Neko a weekly stipend as an
incentive to keep his grades up—and continued to do so all the way
through Neko's college graduation.

There was also a young Blood named Joe who'd been sent to
our program for being a truant his junior year of high school. When
one of our caseworkers met with his teachers and pulled his school
records, however, they discovered that Joe had been a straight-A
student the previous year. I'd seen Joe front and center at several
Tuesday Night Hype sessions, where he'd readily prayed and shared
stories. I met with his mother—she told us that Joe was disrespect-
ful, would not obey her, and only wanted to smoke weed. In our next
meeting with her, she said Joe had left home, was being disruptive;
she wanted to find him in order to turn him over to the authorities.
I eventually found Joe at a friend's house and took him to a nearby
restaurant, where he opened up to me about what was going on for
him at home. He said that his mother didn't want him in the house
because she had a new boyfriend who didn't like Joe. Once, the boyfriend had hit Joe's mother during a fight, and when Joe intervened,
telling him he'd hurt him if he laid a hand on his mother again, his
mother *and* her boyfriend had turned on him. Ultimately, it became
clear that Joe was not going to be comfortable living at home—his
mother continued to make him feel unwelcome—so we connected
him to Job Corps, a career training program for young adults that

offers a place to live while youth learn skills in specific training areas, with the eventual promise of entering the work force or an apprenticeship. Through Job Corps, Joe was able to live and work in San Marcos, Texas, for the summer.

Through our program, I also met a talented sixteen-year-old I'll call K.D. He was an aspiring rapper—but every song in his repertoire was filled to the brim with curse words. His songs also, in my view, romanticized the worst aspects of life in the hood. So I challenged him to perform at Tuesday Night Hype, on the condition that he rap without profanity or a message of misogyny and violence. His first attempt was totally hilarious—he offered original songs and a voice for his generation—but try as he might he plainly *couldn't* replace the swear words that he'd grown accustomed to using in his raps. I challenged him again, sensing how much the culture and his environment had taken hold of him. I asked him to sit down and consciously try to write a song that evoked something less brutal and more loving. I wanted him to visualize—to speak into existence—a different life, one that wasn't filled with drugs and violence and murder.

I took K.D. under my wing and began to mentor him. His father wasn't a part of his life—he'd left the family when K.D. was very young. I like to think that I became somewhat of a father figure for K.D. I also had a soft spot for K.D. because he was the nephew of an old friend of mine—a Blood who'd been murdered years before; K.D. and I bonded over how much we both missed him.

K.D.'s mother and I talked regularly. The two of them lived in dire poverty—frequently, I would help her sort out getting her water turned back on, or I'd bring some food to put in the fridge. K.D.'s mother wanted her son to overcome the inevitable challenges, to not end up on the streets. She was enthusiastic and hopeful, despite her desperate circumstances; we often discussed the improvements she'd seen in her son since he'd joined our program.

Just before K.D. graduated from our program, however, his mother died. Though she'd never let me know it during the time we'd spent together, she'd been battling cancer. It was a difficult blow for K.D. I feared for him. He was very impressionable, and the toxic culture of the neighborhood had gotten so deep in him that taking away the kindness of his mother, I knew, was like severing a lifeline for him. However, even after he graduated our program, he continued to attend Tuesday Night Hype and eventually managed to deliver a positive rap free of curse words. We were all so proud of him that night—everyone threw up their hands and cheered throughout the whole song.

A year later, though, the news reached me that K.D. had been killed while taking part in an armed robbery. It was a sharp loss. We had worked so hard to pull him through after the death of his mother, to offer him an alternate route. It felt like a tragedy that the toxic culture he'd long revered claimed him in the end.

There is always such a long distance to go in this line of work— there are the days when it feels like you're leaving a mark, that the tide is actually turning in the right direction, and then there are the intimate moments of sorrow and frustration, such as this one, when you see that young Black men are still needlessly dying in the prime of their lives.

24

SLANDER

I was signed up to go to a training session led by a police officer from the Gang Unit at the Dallas County Juvenile Department that afternoon; I'd been curious to hear what he had to say regarding young gang members today. I also knew it would be an important collaboration if the two sides—the juvenile probation officers and the police who arrest the kids they work with—were able to have a conversation; I hoped it might help to debunk some of the prejudices I felt some police carry about kids in juvie. But, at the last minute, I realized I had a competing obligation and, disappointed, I let them know I wouldn't be able to make the session after all.

By afternoon, my phone was ringing nonstop. I received call after call from colleagues and friends, telling me that the cop who'd spoken that day had slandered my name at the very juvenile department where I'd been working for years to help teens successfully transition from gang involvement. He'd pointedly asked why they had been working with me and then told them that I was an active gang member; I was recruiting their teens for the 415 Blood gang and to sell drugs; I was, in fact, a drug kingpin under investigation at that very moment. They had raided my mother's house just days earlier, the officer lied, and arrested my cousins. He warned them not to be fooled by my façade—reminding me of the cops who'd alleged to my friends that I was using activism as my cover, putting me under surveillance. He ended by telling the probation officers they should not send their teens to our program unless they wanted to lose them to the streets. But his hateful speech had backfired. I had collaborated with everyone at the juvenile department for years—and now they were enraged. Every single one of them insisted that I sue for defamation of character and offered to testify on my behalf.

I was speechless. I literally couldn't find words to say on the phone to the multitude of people who called to describe what had happened that day. It had been eleven years since I'd been a gang member and nine years since I'd left prison, during which time I'd worked relentlessly to right not just my world again but *the* world. I knew I owed a debt; it was painful and real, and never once had I backed down from it. I'd also encountered, by then, my fair share of critics and naysayers and corruption—and had learned my way around them without losing faith—but *this*, this caught me off guard. As many classes and counseling sessions as I'd held with kids on how to handle their raw anger and disappointment, those lessons were now abruptly turned on me. I had to take a deep breath before I could even think about what to do next.

Once I'd wrapped my mind around what was happening to at least talk about it, I sought advice from Omar. He suggested we go down to headquarters and speak with the officer's superiors about the matter. We discussed how to go about it; I ranted some more. Toward the end of the conversation, Omar looked at me gravely and said, "You must be ready to be arrested if these accusations are true."

"Let's go then," I replied, "because every single one of them is false."

Still, I felt a strong pulse of anxiety. I knew that Omar didn't understand as innately as I did that there was always an unknown variable in this equation—that sometimes innocence has nothing to do with what happens. Corrupt officers were capable of *creating* a situation, able to make an untrue accusation stick if that's what they really wanted. I'd had friends who'd ended up in federal prison just for having appeared in a photo with drug dealers. And I knew that I wasn't exactly popular with the cops, or so I'd been told. But I decided to take the leap of faith necessary to address this head on anyway. I wasn't going to let nearly a decade of meaningful work be trounced by a reckless man.

So Omar and I discovered the names of the co-lieutenants of the gang unit and went to pay them a visit at Dallas Police Department headquarters. When we told them the name of the officer and what he had alleged about me, they were clearly taken aback. They knew about the work Omar and I had been doing with the juvenile department and elsewhere—and they'd never heard anything but praise for us. I began to breathe a little easier, seeing that we had their attention and understanding. I think it also didn't hurt that I mentioned that if I were to sue the police department for slander, more than thirty employees at juvie were willing to testify on my behalf. The two lieutenants were quick to explain that the police officer had acted entirely of his own volition—without the backing of the police department—and he was way out of line. They acknowledged that the officers who had been saying to my friends I was under surveillance had also gone rogue; they'd never been given the authority to do so. One of the lieutenants picked up the phone and called the officer in question—he'd just left the station to work his beat—and asked him to come back to headquarters immediately.

When the officer walked in the room and saw Omar and me, as tough and burly as he was he looked as if he might start sobbing. He was also, it bears mentioning, a Black man. It was not a stereotypical racial incident. I lit into him. "Why did you say I'm under surveillance? That I'm a gang member? That you kicked in the door of my mother's house and arrested my cousins?" Despite my best efforts to keep calm, I bellowed the questions, my voice exploding with the wrath this man had provoked in me. He started sputtering lies, denying he'd said those things, before taking a left turn and saying he'd actually been talking about my past. Everything about his body language, as well as the beads of sweat popping up on his forehead, told me that he was desperately trying to outrun the truth.

"Let me tell you something. If you lie one more time," I said, trying to even out my tone, "I'm going to end this interview. And then I'm going to announce my lawsuit against the Dallas Police Department to all five news stations."

His superiors jumped in, apologizing and reprimanding the officer. They offered to have the Dallas Police Department write an official letter of apology—addressed to the Dallas County Juvenile Department and myself—retracting what the officer had said. In the end, I chose to accept the offer because I knew that the officer didn't represent the entire police department and I strongly believed in the idea of strengthening—not tearing down—the relationship between the police and the community.

The apology and letter, as a gesture, gave me a measure of calm, but it didn't take away the bitter disappointment I felt afterward, that I still feel at times. If that man didn't believe I was sincere, if he

believed I genuinely was a troubling character, I could accept that—
he was allowed his opinion. But the fact that he knowingly spread
false information about me, an officer meant to represent truth and
justice, *that* put me at an interesting intersection. It was a test of my
activism *and* myself: I would have to make the effort to rise above my
own grievances, to move beyond my own grim experience with an
unethical police officer, for the sake of expansive progress.

25

Free at Last, Free at Last

I had never forgotten about Vito sitting in prison for a crime he hadn't committed. The promise I made to him—that I would help him prove his innocence—before I had walked out the prison doors for the last time was etched in my mind. Almost every day since I'd been released, I'd sent an email or talked to or visited a person or organization to plead for help with his case. After many years of searching, a well-known civil attorney whom I'd been referred to by an activist friend recommended that I call a private investigator he knew named Pat. In hindsight, I think he just gave me Pat's number to get rid of me. Nevertheless, I called Pat, and he agreed to meet. When we got together in person, though, after hearing me out for about five minutes, Pat cut me short and said, "Sorry, buddy. I don't do wrongful conviction cases. You need to find someone else." I had been hearing the same answer for about a decade now; it was always a blow. Feeling defeated, I walked slowly back to my car—but something inside me told me to go back. I turned around and soon found myself standing in the hot sun at the window of the guy's car as he was about to pull off, thrusting a sheaf of papers at him.

"Sir, could you please read these trial transcripts? You don't have to promise me anything. As a matter of fact, you don't have to do anything for me except please find the time to read these transcripts." He stared at me for what seemed like an eternity and then just said, "Okay."

Three months later I received a call from Pat. His exact words to me were, "You have an innocent man sitting in prison." He explained that he and his wife, an attorney, had gone to their lake house for the weekend and both had taken the time to read the trial transcripts and police reports I'd given him. I think they had been genuinely moved by what they read, realizing that a sixteen-year-old young man had been put away for a crime that he clearly had not committed. Many details brought them to the conclusion that Vito was innocent, but one in particular stood out: two voir dire witnesses—offering testimony without a jury present—who'd seen the two men before and after the murder took place had indicated that the DA led them to point to Vito as guilty when neither had placed him at the scene of the crime. Pat knew from his work as an investigator that young Black men were often railroaded this way. There was also an enticing financial incentive to take on the case: if he were exonerated, Vito would likely be awarded a couple of million dollars and Pat, as his investigator, would get a percentage of that, in the realm of a couple hundred thousand dollars. I was driven to work on the case partly because Vito and I had a long history but also because I couldn't forget the look on his face, so childlike and terrified, when he had asked me to commit to proving his innocence once I was out of jail.

And so Pat and I began to investigate together how my friend Gary "Vito" Walker had been falsely accused of this horrific crime. To start, we had the two names that Vito had gotten from the inmate who'd told him his friends had killed a woman at Sunchase

Apartments, plus the trial transcripts from Vito's sister Kim that included the police report. Pat started digging into the names and found their criminal records. They both had long and violent records. One of them had been murdered four months after he'd apparently killed the woman at Sunchase; the other had since been sentenced to life in prison for killing someone else. Pat discovered that the guy had a girlfriend and a baby; we believed that if we could find that woman, we might be able to locate the hard evidence we needed to prove that Vito was innocent. We spent months traveling to small towns, knocking on doors, digging up old information in a quest to find the truth.

One day, after months of riding around with Pat, he looked over at me and said, "Man, you would make one hell of a bail bondsmen. You're a man of integrity, good with people, and everyone who knows you speaks highly of you." I vaguely knew what that entailed just from having my own bail set—I understood that bail bondsmen provide written agreements for the courts to pay full bail if the defendant doesn't show up for his trial date; in exchange, families pay 10 percent of the bail to the bondsmen up front. It had never occurred to me as a job I might do though. As it turned out, Pat owned seven bail bond companies throughout the Dallas-Fort Worth metroplex.

A couple of months later, I started a new bail bond business in South Dallas, with Pat as my business partner. This came together at just the right moment for me. With heavy hearts, Omar and I had recently chosen not to renew our contract with the juvenile department. Much as we loved the work, the maze of their bureaucratic system—and having to wind our way through it repeatedly to try to get us, and our staff, paid on time—had proven too difficult. Not to mention that, despite the fact that we had the lowest recidivism rates among our youth of all of the contracted programs in the county, we were the lowest paid. I'd reach a crossroads in my activism that many eventually arrive at: continuing to do it came at the risk of my own financial well-being. I was, in fact, close to losing my house. Had I not happened to know the judge at eviction court, who helped me to negotiate a deal, my house would have been gone already. And by then my kids, Tileyah and Amir, were teenagers—both needed me to be a provider more than the public needed me to be an activist. At the same time, I held out hope that the financial stability of the bond business would give me back the ability to practice my activism.

One day, as I was working in the office, I got a call from a woman who wanted me to look up her son in the system; when she gave me his name, alarm bells went off in my head. He had the same name as the man we'd been investigating in Vito's case, the one who'd purportedly killed the woman at Sunchase and had since been murdered himself. This woman was the girlfriend that Pat and I had been searching for— and here she was, calling me to help bail her son out. I asked for her number and told her I'd get the information she needed and call her right back. I called Pat immediately. "Man, you're not going to believe this," I said as soon as he picked up the phone. We arranged to meet with the woman to discuss her son's bond. When we arrived, Pat explained to her that, yes, we'd be able to help bail her son out, but we had come in person for a different reason. As Pat began to explain the story of the woman who'd been killed at Sunchase, as far as we knew it from Vito and our research, she interrupted. "I was there that night." She had been in the car waiting for her boyfriend at Sunchase that night and was able to corroborate many of the details we'd managed to gather in our investigation. She also told us where to find her boyfriend's accomplice in prison. He, too, after first playing hard, broke down and confessed that his friend had committed the murder.

One year later, in 2012, with my bail bond business doing well, I'd saved enough money to afford to hire a polygrapher, the same one that the Dallas district attorney's office regularly used. Pat had advised that this would be the best next step in securing Vito's freedom. I wasn't sure, however, how it would play out for Vito. The polygrapher was cold and brusque. We sent him to George Beto One Unit unannounced to administer a lie detector test on Vito. Pat and I sat outside the prison for two hours at a barbecue joint, waiting for word of the results. When he finally pulled into the parking lot, I felt a jolt of nerves. This had been a life's mission for me, and I'd come to really care about Vito—I didn't want to learn that my instincts had been entirely wrong. The polygrapher got out of his car and, with a completely unreadable expression on his face, walked up to us. "That's an innocent man."

With that, Pat and I went to the Texas Parole Board on behalf of Vito and presented them with the new evidence we had gathered. Prior to this, every time Vito had been presented to the parole board and was asked to accept responsibility for his crime—a proforma question asked of all prisoners up for parole—Vito had declined to do so. We explained that a man couldn't claim responsibility, or show remorse, for a crime he'd never committed. Later that month, they voted to release Vito on parole while we furthered the process of proving his innocence. Picking Vito up from the Walls Unit releasing center in Huntsville and hearing him utter the words, "Free at last, free at last," as he pushed open the heavy metal door will always be one of the greatest joys, and triumphs, of my life.

It was, it seemed, a time of momentous exits and entrances. A month later, my grandmother called to tell me that my father was also being released from prison. She asked me to go pick him up that afternoon. Stunned, I agreed and hung up the phone, a million questions racing through my mind. *What do I say to him? After thirty-six years, do I still call him* Dad? *Do I hug him or shake his hand? Do I ask him why? Have I truly forgiven?* As all these questions were rising, my anger also began to surge. I started to think about my stepfather, how, in the absence of my father, he'd beat me when I was little. I thought about how hard my mother always had to work and all the things I did for my son that my own father had never done for me.

As I neared the release center, I determined that I would shake my father's hand and be standoffish because, after all, I didn't know him. My whole life prior to that point had been as the child of an incarcerated man, and I felt I was too old for a daddy at that point. When I got out of the car, my stomach flipped as I looked around the men who were exiting the holding facility. Then I spotted him wearing the same old shabby clothes I had worn leaving prison, looking wide-eyed and hopeful. He noticed me, and as he started to run, I had to grit my teeth to hold back the tears welling up. The little boy in me wanted to run to meet him, but the man in me was holding back. The boy won. I moved quickly toward him, and he picked me up in a bear hug and wouldn't let me go. He said, "I love you, man" and it was as if a pipe burst in me. I cried uncontrollably, and it became me who wouldn't let him go. We stood there in our embrace for three minutes—but it seemed like thirty-six years. When we had both brought our emotions under control, I stood back and said, "Pops, let's go get some soul food."

Free at last, free at last. Thank God Almighty, we are free at last.

26

URBAN SPECIALIST

Michael Brown did not have a criminal record, never got into trouble with juvie, and, by his mother's account, was never in a gang either. In these respects, he was unlike many of the kids I'd worked with or even who I'd been myself—but his life ended in a way that had become plainly familiar to all of us. On August 9, 2014, about a week after graduating from high school, eighteen-year-old Brown, suspected of stealing a box of Swisher Sweets cigars from the Ferguson Market in a suburb of St. Louis, Missouri, was shot at least eight times by police officer Darren Wilson. The entirety of their encounter lasted about a minute and a half.

After the now well-known Ferguson uprising—protests and riots that took place after Michael Brown's killing, advancing a reckoning for the American police—Omar and I realized the value of our decade and a half of activism and how we might bring it to bear in these circumstances. We were ready to expand our activism to take on a national tragedy and the issue of police brutality.

Right away, Omar and I led a rally to ask for accountability in policing at the Martin Luther King Jr. community center, strategically speaking in front of Dr. King's statue. Amir and Tileyah were there, front and center, in the MY LIFE HAS VALUE Too t-shirts I'd bought for them. Looking at them in the crowd, I felt immense anger and fear as a father—Wilson had clearly not valued Michael Brown's life—but I also knew that indicting the entire police department would be a mistake. Even during my own standoff with the police officer who had maligned my name and reputation, I'd kept myself from regarding the department as one monolithic idea, wholly culpable for the reckless actions of one of its members. I had also, however, been stripped of the notion that all policemen are the moral authorities we once expected them to be; some, I knew, could be monsters. Beyond that, it was the same point I had been trying to get police officers to understand about our young men in communities: not all of them are criminals.

At that rally, many young activists were gathered who'd just become conscious of civic responsibility. They were, understandably, furious and shaken. They spoke up aggressively—against the police, against the violence, against the torment. As I watched, I realized that this was a crucial early stage of activism—turning up the volume on a serious problem and making your voice heard. There is power in this, and it plays a valuable role in demanding attention, but I also knew deep in my bones that, in order to truly move the needle, we would have to take a more nuanced approach. I recalled that when I'd first started my work with Omar and was meeting with members of the Bloods to try to dispel gang violence, they were only willing to hear me out if I would "go tell the Crips the same thing, because every time we see them, they're still advancing on us." The same lesson, and principle, was at play here: these protests were a step in the right direction, but if we were going to funnel this energy toward purpose and action we had to engage both sides and start having the difficult conversations that would give more distinct shape not only to the problems but also to the solutions.

With that in mind, Omar and I, now having incorporated the work of Vision Regeneration into a new organization called Urban Specialists, with a small staff that included Vito, began to focus our work on systemic changes. Our first move was to teach the kids in our community, mainly through an afterschool program, about what is formally termed *compliance*—but really means imparting the blunt reality that Black kids, as a matter of survival, need to know how to keep an interaction with the police from escalating. At that time, the national narrative was focused on the police, but we strongly felt that in order not to see any more of these kids become statistics or hashtags, we had to hit the ground running with the younger generation first. We borrowed the Dallas County Public Defender's Office guide on how to create a lesson about a safe range of responses when stopped by the police—keep your hands on the steering wheel if stopped while driving your car; remain calm; don't talk back or act belligerent.

It was a delicate balance, instilling the lesson of safety while also not belittling the positive contributions of the police department, particularly as issues around the police had become so contentious in the news and on social media. Now that people were able to capture some of their more shocking actions on video with their phones, many kids had internalized the message that all cops were villains. To counter *that* narrative, we invited local police officers to visit our afterschool program. In fact, we started by having them come in their plain clothes to act as mentors to the kids. At the end of the session, once they'd had time to bond, we'd reveal to the kids that the mentors were also police officers. We felt that by bringing them into personal contact and facilitating a relationship, it would be harder to have a fatal interaction down the road. These efforts were aimed at puncturing the broad prejudices—that all Black kids are menacing; that all cops are bad—that many had thoughtlessly clung to for so long.

Once we mediated a conversation between two police officers and our kids; emotions were high in that exchange, the kids broadly denouncing the police as intimidating and harmful. Swept up by the passion of their exchange, I pointed to one of the officers, an older Black woman, and, surprised at my own fervor, shouted, "This lady right here, I'm willing to bet that she became a police officer because she wanted to help her community. And she probably does a great job. But under this new narrative that says all police officers are antagonists, now when she interacts with the community she loves, it's a hostile situation." I was a little embarrassed that I had spoken for her—I had no idea if what I'd just said was true—but after the discussion was over, she gave me a hug. "How did you know that?" she asked.

The police leadership training sessions we began doing, in partnership with the Carruth Police Institute and the Dallas Police Department, called "How to Engage the Community," was a natural evolution from that work. We were tasked with facilitating conversations about implicit biases. So I started the meetings with a picture of myself in my prison uniform projected onto the wall. I gave no explanation; I just let the officers sit with the image for the first five minutes before I walked into the room. I knew some of them would make a judgment based on the image and hold it in mind about me as I walked in to lead the session. I *wanted* to elicit that prejudice in them. I sometimes even saw grimaces pass over some faces when I, the inmate on the screen they'd been sitting with, walked in and explained that I was one of the original founders of the 415 Bloods. But I also knew that, ultimately, I could convince them that transformation is possible and real. We judge based on cues and assumptions, eroding our goodwill and relationships, but that usually ceases to be an option when you're engaged in intimate conversation. After all, it's hard to hate up close.

The years immediately following Michael Brown only brought more grievous news of needless Black deaths at the hands of errant police officers. Shortly after Brown died, Tamir Rice, twelve years old, was shot and killed by an officer in Cleveland, Ohio, for playing with a toy gun in public. In 2015, researchers found that young Black men were *nine* times more likely than other Americans to be killed by a police officer. In 2016, within a day of each other, Alton Sterling, a thirty-seven-year-old Black father of five, in Baton Rouge, Louisiana, and Philando Castile, a thirty-two-year-old African American stopped for a traffic violation while driving with his partner and her five-year-old daughter in a suburb of St. Paul, Minnesota, were brutally killed by police officers.

On July 7, 2016, during a protest in Dallas over the deaths of both those men, Micah Xavier Johnson, an African American war veteran who was angry about the seemingly endless massacre of Black men, went on his own shooting spree, killing five police officers and injuring nine others. And, suddenly, the violence spurred by the escalating racial tensions in our nation had landed in our own backyard. The chief of police reached out to Omar and me for help; the city was on the brink of rioting. We moved quickly and called for a closed-door meeting with all the community activists, leaders, politicians, and police we could gather. We intentionally didn't invite the media because we had learned, having conducted many of these types of meetings with gang and community members, that participants needed the privacy and space to be vulnerable.

It was a troubling, and terrifying, moment for everyone. The racially motivated violence—once at least offering the delicate silver lining of stirring strong-willed activism—now seemed instead to be creating an expectation of more violence. It was the biggest challenge that Omar and I had faced in our years of working together, but we also saw it as our greatest opportunity.

There were people from every side of the equation in the room—Black activists, white police, pro-police politicians, anti-police community members. And they were all extremely distraught. Within minutes, they were at each other's throats, battling as if their lives depended on it. I can honestly say it was not only one of the most hostile situations I'd ever been in—and lord knows I'd been in plenty of hostile situations—but it was also one of bleakest. On one side, among the activists and anti-police faction, there was a tally going on—a body count from history—for all the people the Black community had wretchedly and unfairly lost at the hands of police officers. The unspoken final point of their message was: *So that's the least that you should suffer, five officers dead. Now you know how we feel.* The police officers and some of the politicians, on the other hand, were brittle and defensive; they hadn't killed those people; they all but said they were serving to *protect* the community.

I spoke that day, and Omar led us in prayer. We offered the message we'd been honing throughout our work together, one that seemed uniquely suited to this moment. They all had every right to be angry, of course. They *should* be angry. We were all grieving—and anger is an important early stage of traumatic loss. Following that, we might feel the next stages of grief: bargaining and depression and acceptance. But there are two more stages in *activism*: together, we need to enter into righteous purpose and, after that, strategic public action. We cannot remain in anger, Omar and I told the group. That will only, in the end, hurt us. When we move forward from fury, we reach both purpose and faith. And only then will things change.

27

━━◆━━

UNLIKELY COLLABORATORS

Not long after Omar and I felt we'd hit our stride, bringing a kaleidoscopic view to our activism, we received a series of surprising professional invitations. Each one brought us the support—professionally, emotionally, or financially, sometimes all three at once—we needed to enlarge our view of the work and scale our activism. In 2015, for instance, we found ourselves in a private meeting in Washington, DC, with then speaker of the house Paul Ryan, along with about fifteen other members of small nonprofit organizations from around the country, to discuss Grassroots Solutions to Poverty.

The year prior, Paul had declared that the War on Poverty launched by President Lyndon Johnson a half century ago was not working. To that end, he released a two-hundred-plus-page report that compared the size and scope of the government's efforts to tackle poverty—stating that ninety-two federal programs aimed at low-income people had cost $799 billion per year—against the results. "For too long, we have measured compassion by how much we spend instead of how many people get out of poverty," he explained, sounding a lot like Bob Woodson. "We need to take a hard look at what the federal government is doing and ask, 'Is this working?'"

In fact, Bob Woodson had recently accompanied Paul Ryan on a listening and learning tour of low-income neighborhoods throughout the U.S.—which is how we'd found our way to this activist conference table with Paul Ryan at the head. Woodson had assembled us to advise the speaker of the house about programs that were already working to combat poverty, as well to suggest possible reforms for the current welfare system, as research for a proposal he would unveil the following year.

After Paul spoke to the group, he opened the conversation for questions. I raised my hand and reflected back to him his proposition to give states the ability to make decisions related to welfare benefits—allowing, as he'd said, the government to be "a one-stop shop." I respectfully disagreed. My concern was that state's rights in the Black community sounded too much like Confederate rights. I wanted him to understand that a state like Texas, for example, because of its history, hadn't made it as far as some of the more progressive states. Black people were still being indiscriminately penalized; allowing the Texas state government to determine when a segment of its population should or shouldn't get welfare would necessarily overlook a decent amount of complexity; it would almost certainly be a challenge for a fair system to emerge. To his credit, Ryan nodded and said he hadn't seen it that way and that he'd like to hear more. After the meeting, Paul met with Omar and me so that we could expand on our ideas and suggestions—and he continued to be in touch with us from then on to get our input and to give us support. I was surprised at how easily Paul brought us into his fold and how consistently he sought our opinion. I hadn't expected much more than a handshake and group conversation when Bob had invited us to meet with him. I would soon find that Paul's influence would wend its way into our lives in more subtle ways too, opening doors that I might never have even known existed.

A year after we first met Paul, Omar and I were invited to a conference—with the intriguing name of *Unlikely Collaborators*—in Ojai, California. As we drove in from the airport, past mountains and long stretches of lush, grassy fields, I had a vision of other similar landscapes I'd seen. Though they hadn't come anywhere close to the magnificence of this one, I couldn't help but think of the manicured lawn and rolling hills of Glen Mills, as well as the eerie drive to Beto, with those enormous trees that seemed to loom in warning of the experience to come. Those earlier vistas were connected to sinister places in my mind, though I'd managed to wring the best I could out of both of them. This expanse of nature, however, made me feel a pure connection to my larger purpose; it seemed to suggest that the world would keep opening to me.

Unlikely Collaborators created tools and experiences—including workshops, ongoing community sessions, and storytelling events— that guided people to investigate their own stories, to discover what self-defeating thought patterns and unconscious blocks might lie within. And to expand those narratives in ways that allow them to thrive, to nurture supportive relationships, and ultimately build a more compassionate, radiant world. There were discussions and workshops about cognitive distortions, perception boxes, and unconscious beliefs; there were investigations of people's own stories and expansive conversations about the self-defeating thought patterns that are operating below the conscious. The woman at the center of this gathering—I learned that first night when she addressed the crowd with a captivating speech—was Elizabeth Koch, author, entrepreneur and daughter of the CEO of Koch Industries, Charles Koch. I hesitate even to mention Charles Koch here because Elizabeth has done so much good and successful work beyond her formidable family name and has created her own distinct, inclusive presence. For me, the work resonated well with the work I had done in prison with men trying to identify with what led us there in the first place. The whole weekend felt nostalgic to me. I knew I was there for a divine reason. It was an amazing weekend generally. More specifically, I left that conference with a new and unexpected mentor. Elizabeth has offered me so much—friendship, collaboration, understanding—but, mainly, I've learned from her to try to turn the same insight and forgiveness that I offer in my activism toward myself. It's a circular arrangement anyway: If I'm able to feel the full capacity of my own strength and power, I have that much more of it to give to the world.

Not even a year after our trip to Ojai, Omar and I were called back to California. This time, to a summit in Palm Springs called A Time to Lead with five hundred of the world's wealthiest business leaders and philanthropists. Omar hadn't told me much more than that about the event, so I was expecting something more corporate, maybe a bit more conventional than our usual settings. Instead, as we drove up the winding driveway, a couple of men looking like high-end bodyguards in black suits with earpieces received us, checking for our names on their lists. They took our cellphones, sealing them in bags, before we entered a lavish ballroom. Inside was a sea of somewhere around five hundred of the most impeccably dressed white folks I'd ever seen.

"Man, is this the Illuminati?" I whispered jokingly to Omar as we walked in.

As it turned out, it was a conference hosted by Charles Koch himself, bringing together some of America's most powerful leaders to discuss their charitable efforts and organizations. They were gathered to give a variety of presentations, but Omar and I zeroed in on the one about criminal justice reform. We'd actually had some affiliation with Charles Koch prior to this. We'd met his daughter by then, of course, but she hadn't played a role in our being there. Even before our paths had crossed with Elizabeth, Omar and I had met Evan Feinberg, the executive director of Stand Together, a nonprofit founded by Charles to provide financial support to organizations working to improve education, business, communities, and government. Evan had been very interested in the work we were doing and had continued the conversation with Omar, eventually offering some funding to Urban Specialists. And yet Omar didn't think that Evan was the reason we were now mingling in Palm Springs either. His hunch was that Paul Ryan had mentioned our work to Charles Koch. We may never know quite how we ended up there—cloaked in secrecy as the process seems to be—but then, we weren't too worried about *how* we'd gotten there once we were there. We were more focused on what was to come.

Omar and I spent the next three days attending talks and then breaking down into smaller groups to discuss and network. The speakers were well versed in their respective areas; in the ballroom presentation on criminal justice reform, for instance, the presenter spoke at a granular level about the sentencing disparity in the United States for possession of crack cocaine—used in greater numbers by Black Americans—and powder cocaine—used far more by whites. And yet Black Americans are sentenced to prison for twice the amount of time as their white counterparts caught with powder cocaine. They were discussing how we fix this broken system that disproportionately penalizes people of color. Meantime, the predominant image of the drug offender in the media is that of people like I used to be—gang members hanging around the dark alleys of the hood. It was strange and fascinating to not just see this other world—made up of the mythic one percent—but also to see how they were seeing me.

I had never encountered activism at this level before. I'd had my brushes with wealth with Don Williams or at other meetings with Bob Woodson, but I'd never seen it in this concentrated form. And yet, I found that at this lofty height, the ambition and aim was similarly direct: let's work to remove barriers to upward mobility for those at the bottom. I was exhilarated, actually, to find a community that had both the resources *and* influence to put into an effort so similar to ours—and to change the world.

After a decade and a half as an activist, I had sought help from federal programs, local politicians, national politicians, religious institutions, and affluent clergy in order to help the people I knew were in need. Occasionally, we'd found a philanthropist with a heart who wanted to help with a particular issue that sparked his or her interest. But I had never before encountered someone like Charles Koch—towering, divisive figure in the world that he may be—who had been as seriously and enduringly supportive of our work *and* of me. Proximity helped me see a genuine, principled man with a heart to do good in the world who I learned to admire.

Omar and I wanted to bring the conversations that we had been convening and evolving since Michael Brown's death—from the kids who we'd taught compliance, to the officers with whom I'd tried to dismantle prejudice, to the fiery confrontations between the community and the police—to a national stage. Vulnerable, human exchange had become the cornerstone of our activism, and those disruptive conversations were, we felt, the surest routes to genuine change. Electrifying, high-wire interactions, allowing for broad and varying points of view, force people out of their safe corners into a place where they become alive to ideas that they may not otherwise allow themselves to consider. It may create a reasonable doubt about long-held opinions in some; it may harden abiding beliefs in others. Either way, it makes us think about the people we are living with, perhaps on the far end of the political or socioeconomic or cultural spectrum but side-by-side, nonetheless.

In 2018, on Martin Luther King's birthday—fifty years after his tragic assassination—we held our first Course Correction conversation in Dallas. It brought together a diverse array of leaders to discuss racial violence, particularly as it related to police shootings. We recruited as wide a range of people who'd been affected by the issue as we could conceive, with the aim to illuminate it from all angles. We assembled elder civil rights leaders, young activists, hip-hop organizers, and police representatives. Reverend Bernice King, the CEO of the Martin Luther King Jr. Center for Nonviolent Social Change and the youngest daughter of Dr. Martin Luther King Jr., sat on stage with, among others, Republican Senator Ted Cruz; the rapper Scarface; Sybrina Fulton, mother of Trayvon Martin, the seventeen-year old African American boy fatally shot in 2012 while walking home from a 7-Eleven in Sanford, Florida, wearing the hoodie that has since become a symbol of solidarity and carrying a bag of Skittles with a can of iced tea; former track and field athlete John Carlos, who famously held up his fist in a Black Power salute at the 1968 Summer Olympics while on the podium to accept

the bronze medal in the two hundred meters; Democratic Congresswoman Eddie Bernice Johnson; NFL Hall of Famer Deion Sanders;
Andricka Williams, the mother of Alton Sterling's children, as well
as Tonja Garafola and Trenisha Jackson, wives of two slain police officers in Baton Rouge, shot in the wake of Sterling's death. This event
allowed us to start a much-needed national dialogue about the bitter
divide in our country. We are all Americans. The urban youth killed
without just cause are Americans. The police are Americans. It may
sound naive or simplistic but it's also unavoidably true: we need to
learn to coexist. "We can live together as brothers," as Dr. King once
said, "or die alone as fools."

The Course Correction conversations led us to the notion that
we could create a kind of traveling discourse employing Dr. King's
principles of nonviolence and activating weapons to win love and
redemption—inviting in a new mix of thought leaders throughout—
to keep pushing for innovative change, while also giving rise to an
unexpected community. "God gave me an idea!" I recall Omar crying
out with his characteristic enthusiasm, when it first occurred to him
that we should create this kind of traveling show of democracy. "We
need to heal America from its divide. We need to do a Heal America
tour!"

And so we did just that, taking Heal America: A Course Correction Conversation on Race, Citizenship & Humanity on the road
in 2019. As it turned out, it was a sorrowfully prescient idea. Though
it already felt as if we were addressing a profoundly fractured nation as we set out to have this roving conversation, zigzagging from
Dallas to Detroit to Minnesota to Atlanta to Chicago, we had yet
to experience the overwhelming murders of more innocent Black
Americans—Elijah McClain, walking home from a convenience

store, Ahmaud Arbery, jogging in his own neighborhood, Breonna Taylor, sleeping in her bed, and, of course, George Floyd, killed after allegedly using a counterfeit twenty-dollar bill to buy cigarettes. It seemed these devastations were only coming faster and with more ferociousness, deepening the impassioned protests of the Black Lives Matters movement and arguably creating the sharpest political and societal divide felt since the American Civil Rights movement was born more than half a century ago. It steeply challenged our sense that we could find a way to reach across the ever-deepening schism of our country, but we pressed on, believing that this form of compassionate activism was the only way.

Like it or not, we are all in this together, with vastly different circumstances and feelings, with infinite variations on the same theme: how can we create a just world? At the end of the day, these difficult conversations are inescapable. But the more often we have them, the more we see humanity from all sides; the more complicated it becomes but also the more conceivable it is that we will be presented with decent possibilities for living together. We cannot change the injustices of history—they will echo always from the past—but we *can* move forward with the startling promise of human connection.

I am aware of how difficult it is to get there. I can still raise the old rage at the cop who slandered me; I can feel shaky with grief at how much harder I have had to work, as a Black person, in prison and out of it, *and* as an activist. Yet I also know I have to push myself to reach beyond those feelings, for my sake as much as for others— because this is the only way that lasting progress is made.

Ironically, prison allowed me to address a generational trauma that had long been unfolding in my own life—and begin to heal. In recognizing that I'd inherited both the experiences of my father *and* my race, that I'd, at least in part, been delivered to these circumstances by an invisible force of history, I was able to begin stripping back the protective layers of my own being. And I found the essential humanity at my core. This made me more vulnerable than I'd ever been, but also more powerful; I was now open for true connection. I no longer saw the tattoos covering an inmate's face, or his threatening snarl. I saw his armor, and I knew that he, too, was buried under the debris of fear and pain that I had been, that we *all* are. And when I reached out to him with a sense of compassion, eventually he was able to meet me with the one thing we all have in common: grace.

Activism, too, must be generous in this way. Because when it condemns in any direction—as, truth be told, it sometimes does—it has already gotten in its own way. Without endeavoring for redemption—maintaining an unceasing belief in the capacity for change in all humans—we are simply chasing our own tails. It can be crushing to glimpse what looks like the cyclical nature of history—to see it as a succession of unflinching, unchanging injustices from the Red Summer of 1919 to the lynching of Emmett Till to the final breaths of George Floyd, pinned under the knee of a police officer. Alongside these heart-wrenching sacrifices of human life, however, there is also a line to be drawn from Frederick Douglass to Harriet Tubman to Martin Luther King to Rosa Parks to Bishop Omar. But, perhaps most crucially, the collective advance of history is not direct. It takes us forward, then pulls us back, then catapults farther in the direction of progress once more. But always, this forward movement is propelled by the dynamic energy of compassion. It is up to us, then, to reveal the best of ourselves, the essential decency of humankind, to shape the days to come.

ACKNOWLEDGMENTS

———◆———

I would like to acknowledge my mother, Inez Lucky, for giving me the wonderful blessing of life. She is my driving force to become more than what society deemed for a kid growing up in the projects. Her constant and often harsh challenge for me to be better never left my tiny soul. I thank you kindly and feel honored to have you as my mother. I acknowledge my grandmother and grandfather Emit and Thelma Lucky; in their absence, I am applying the principles they instilled in me many moons ago. I acknowledge my children D'Andrea, Tileyah, and Amir for making me human and accountable to life's demands. You made me kill those selfish desires I had hidden underneath all the gunk and armor. I love you immensely for that. I am honored to have my siblings Adrian (Big A), Booker T (Moon), Michael (Mike-Mike), and baby sister ShaThelma (Shay Shay). I was the only child, and then you all showed up and took that away from me, but I love each of you immensely. Andrea, Markesha, and Kenyada, I am forever indebted to you for your patience with my growth cycles and for how you all each contributed to my success. My peculiar family, the Luckys: without your love in the most desperate of times (especially Rainbo, Super Dave, and K-Ray), I don't think I'd be here today. My best friend, Clay Rider, and my brothers Tiger and Keke: our friendship stood the test of time.

My friend list is too extensive to add here, but those who walked through the valley of death with me, and those who met me on the other side and can bear witness to the transformation, I thank you. I have had many mentors along the way who poured into me, and just like my friends, they are too many to name. I give special thanks to Nia Khepera and Amon Rashidi for igniting the spark. I am utterly thankful to the C. W. Fleming family and my prison-to-freedom mentor and big brother Willie Ray Fleming. I met Willie in 1997 inside prison, and when I tell you the impact that connection had on my life, I am forever grateful and credit him with my trajectory even until today and beyond. He taught me valuable lessons in a place where valuable lessons were scarce. He prepared me for the divine connection with my free-world soul-tie brother Bishop Omar Jahwar. This book is dedicated to Bishop Omar Jahwar because of his huge impact on my life. There aren't enough words to describe it. We toiled together on this road and fought to bring this idea of redemption for the marginalized to fruition. In doing so, we discovered that each and every human being is entitled to it.

I embarked on this journey a few years ago, but I kept stopping. Then I was blessed to meet this wonderful soul who fueled my courage to complete this assignment. She was in tears after hearing a part of my story, and without hesitation said, "I am going to help you share your story with the world." In that instant we became soul-tied. Her name is Elizabeth Koch. I thank you, Elizabeth, because it was you who taught me to free myself of those cognitive distortions that kept me from continuing this book. It was you who taught me how to understand and jump freely out of my perception box. Before you, I didn't know what a perception box was. We are both from the same exact stardust particles. You are my she-ro! Thank you to my editor, Mensah Demary, who challenged my thinking and kept pushing me further. Thank you to everyone who believed in me. Hopefully, after reading this book, you will bear witness to transformation and redemption up close and personal. You will see a kid born with so much potential suffocated by an idea that valued survival and toughness over education and principles, who takes a hard fall but finds within him the wherewithal to turn it all around. *A Redemptive Path Forward* is not only a personal memoir, but also a roadmap for the future of our country.

ANTONG LUCKY is an activist, advocate, and public speaker concentrating in the areas of mentoring Black men and boys, bridging the gap between community and police, and developing and launching violence reduction strategies, criminal justice reform, and reentry initiatives for formerly incarcerated people. Find out more at AntongSpeaks.com.